HOW TO CREATE & SELL DIGITAL PRODUCTS

P TEAGUE

CONTENTS

1. Why Create & Sell Digital Products?   1
2. My Product Creation Experience   11
3. Digital Formats & Terminology   24
4. Essential Tools for Digital Product Creation   33
5. Digital Product Creation Tips & Techniques   38
6. Backup, Storage and Simple Product Delivery   50
7. Going It Alone with Product Delivery   58
8. Digital Sales Platforms   68
9. Outsourcing   78
10. Strategies to Boost Digital Product Sales   84
11. Membership Sites & Tiered Product Launches   97
12. Affiliate Marketing   108
13. Product Support Options   116
14. Presentation tools   122
15. Digital Product Creation Next Steps   128

About the Author   135

WHY CREATE & SELL DIGITAL PRODUCTS?

I built my first web page for personal use in 2002. It was a simple, one-page affair announcing the birth of our third child. The moment that page went live and was available for all the world to see, something fired in me. I had been tapping away at a computer which was squashed into the corner of our landing just at the top of the stairs. This involved using a dial-up connection on an old computer that we'd been given in a throw-out at work. But there I was, sending out digital content into the world, using only free or cheap materials, from the top of our staircase.

The possibilities of the web have intoxicated me ever since. At the time, I was in charge of a new web team in my day job at the BBC without a clue about how to make websites. But the BBC trained me up, showing me how to use Dreamweaver, Photoshop, Flash (remember that?) and RealPlayer. The more I learned, the quicker I was to catch on. Going digital placed a global power at our fingertips, and I wanted a piece of the action. Creating that one-page website was my first effort at harnessing the immense potential of going digital. It took me a few years until I was able to learn how to turn that into digital product launches which were capable of making six-figure sales.

There has never been a better time to create and sell digital products, whether you're new to running your business or you've been at it for years. If you've never run a business of your own, this is the way to do it. I even tell my own kids not to work for somebody else. I advise them to create and sell digital products, it's the way to go as far as I'm concerned. And if you've been in business for years already? That's more than fine too. You have experience, expertise, existing customers and credibility. You don't even have to begin from a standing start, you can easily pivot into this high-profit digital world. I was part of a mastermind group once alongside a vet who was making so much money from his digital sales that he gave up his premises and customer-facing work altogether, in favour of online training products and web-based CPD (continuing professional development), in the UK.

The global Covid-19 pandemic demonstrated just how precarious old-fashioned bricks-and-mortar businesses can be. Supply chains for physical products were quickly disrupted, shops swiftly pivoted to selling online, and anybody whose job required their presence had to down tools. In the meantime, those selling digital products – such as ebooks, online training courses, software services and audio files – continued to sell, uninterrupted. Their shops stayed open to customers throughout the world, many of them generated more income than ever before and it was all done from the comfort of their kitchen table without ever having to leave the house.

There is something very compelling about this vision to me. It is the perfect way to make a living or pivot from an existing business as far as I am concerned. Creating and selling digital products is an option that is open to you regardless of geographical location, disability, age or education. You can start from scratch or you can move your existing business in a new direction entirely to incorporate this technique. If you have access to a computer and internet connection you can build an amazing online business, selling products all over the world and generating thousands of pounds in income from products which don't even exist. You can't even hold a digital product – it exists in cyberspace. No postal delivery service is required, you never run low on stock and people can pay you in any currency they want, including cryptocurrency if you know what to do with it.

I have specifically excluded physical products from the title of this book. I'm not interested in selling goods that you can hold. I include CDs, DVDs, Blu-ray discs and anything else that you can touch in that definition too. Products like these require suppliers, postal delivery systems, storage space, profit margins, returns and supply chains. That's too much like hard work. I'm more interested in creating a digital business that is open for business 24/7, that sells high-profit products which you can't even touch, and which allows me to generate income while I'm sleeping. However, I will be discussing POD – print-on-demand – and how you can use it to sell books. If all that sounds like a great way to make a living, you're in the right place. Read on, I'll tell you exactly how it's done and why, in the 21st century, you must consider this as an income generation strategy.

Low production costs

The immediate beauty of digital products is their low production costs. Much of the time they can be created using free or very low-cost tools. Once you've assembled the kit you need to get started, the biggest outlay is your time.

Just compare that to opening up your own shop. Before you make a penny, you have to lease a store and that in turn obligates you to business rates and utility costs. Next, you have to fit out the premises, advertise your enterprise and stock the shelves. In stocking up, you have to lay out considerable expenses which will be tied up in unsold products until you start making sales; it's 'dead' cash until the item sells. You may have very high equipment costs, particularly if you're opening a restaurant or other food-serving premises. All of this is before you even start recruiting staff and training them. Oh, and then there are the very high costs of advertising your new business, an expense that will be ongoing if you want to keep customers coming through the door.

Phew! It makes me tired just thinking about it. Why does anybody even set up a physical business these days? There is so much financial risk and exposure, it makes me shudder just thinking about it.

Consider the maximum costs of setting up a digital products business, and as you'll find as you progress through this book, these really are exaggerated expenses. Here's my imaginary shopping list:

- Laptop = £300
- Software allowance = £300

Have you ever seen a shorter shopping list? There aren't even enough items there to call it a list. And that software allowance is generous. I can recommend free products to you which will help you to avoid those costs altogether. So, at the very most, I'm proposing a maximum expense of £600 for a business which is capable of making you that amount of money in a single day. It's made me more money than that in an hour in the past, but I want to keep your expectations reasonable and anchored; there were a specific set of circumstances which allowed me to make sales at that fast rate. And yes, I will explain how it's done.

Having a business which affords you low production costs, means it's easier to make a profit. Physical stores are draining cash before you even draw breath. They take a massive amount of capital up front and it's very unlikely that you'll be able to pay that back over a short time period. With digital sales, the production expenses are so low, it's very hard not to recoup the costs, which are mainly in time spent anyway, and it's so much easier to generate profit as a result. Profits with digital products can be in excess of 90% after you take payment processor fees into account. The money you make after those small expenses are paid out goes to determine what will be a very high hourly rate for you as the product creator. We don't do minimum wage when we sell digital products.

Worldwide distribution

One of the business models I considered more recently was selling physical products via Amazon or eBay. This has become quite a fad in recent times, and it was a model to which I gave serious consideration. However much I looked at it, it simply didn't stack up against digital-only sales and the single biggest problem and business weakness was in the worldwide distribution requirements.

This model usually involves sourcing profitable products via Alibaba in China, having them shipped to EU, UK or US distribution centres and then having Amazon (FBA or

Fulfilment by Amazon) or eBay deliver them from there. It's a very profitable model too, which is why I seriously considered it, but it also has several vulnerabilities. The moment you get involved in out-of-country distribution, you're caught up in international and supply chain issues. There are taxes involved, inspection costs, potential damage and loss scenarios, supply chain interruption potential and vulnerability to strikes, and customs and political issues.

None of that applies to digital products. The worst that can happen is that you may have to charge VAT at the standard rate that is levied in the country of sale, but I'm going to explain to you how you can completely – and legally, I hasten to add – mitigate that issue.

Digital products get downloaded via internet connections, there are no lorries, no customs officials and no supply chain dependencies. The worst thing that can happen is that the broadband goes off; if that ever happens, I suspect things will be so bad you won't be bothered about your internet business by that stage anyway.

Endless inventory

Have you tried to buy a product and it's out of stock? Frustrating, isn't it? It means somebody's supply chain was interrupted, a member of staff hasn't got a grip of supply and demand levels or there's some other spanner in the works.

This never happens with digital products because they only exist in a somewhat ethereal form on a server. If you ever see a digital service 'closed down' or 'full', you're simply watching an effective sales strategy, known as 'scarcity', in action. A digital product can't be 'sold out' it's impossible. Once it's created and uploaded to the server, it's an instant delivery automated sales machine. I say that without even the slightest hint of reservation. As I'm typing these words, I am selling my books at the rate of more than once every five minutes due to a rather effective promotion I've got running. This stuff works and when it does, running out of inventory will never be a problem for us.

High perceived value

Digital products have a high perceived value. I have paid five thousand pounds for online training in the past and on more than one occasion.There are some exceptions to this; interestingly, as a fiction author, buyers of my books seem not to attribute a high value to fiction ebooks. However, start writing non-fiction and begin to provide information or educational products, and the price goes up immediately. There's a reason for this which I'll discuss in more detail later in the book. In simple terms, the buyer wants what I've got, and they're prepared to pay me for it. In the case of this book, it's information. There's nothing here you can't find out for yourself on YouTube. When you buy this book, you're paying for almost two decades of online experience, distilled into a digest of actionable information. You're accessing my hours of learning, my years of experience selling thousands of digital products throughout the world, you're accessing knowledge I paid thousands of pounds to secure. It's pretty cheap at less than £10 when you put it like that.

The alternative is to track it down on the internet, going up blind alleys, taking wrong turns and making mistakes along the way. The simple truth is that people are prepared to pay for knowledge; it's the quickest and most painless way to go from A-Z, and for that customers will pay you well to access your skills and experience.

Evergreen content

I'll let you into a secret: I've sold the information in this book many times in multiple formats. That is not to diminish its value, the knowledge I share in this book is worth every penny. If you follow the guidance I give here, you could turn the £10 cost of the paperback into thousands of pounds. It's the method I'm using to share this information that has changed this time around.

One of the lessons I learned through painful experience is that the trick to creating the most profitable digital products is in making them timeless and future-proof. When I first started writing non-fiction books, I wrote them about topics which dated quickly. I was producing ebooks about LinkedIn, Twitter and Facebook, yet those platforms seemed to change every five minutes, meaning my books constantly needed updating.

This book has been produced as an evergreen product; that is, one

that will not date quickly. I have placed resources on a special page at Create-Digital-Products.com and that means I can update a web page if something changes, rather than having to rewrite and republish an entire book.

It's crucial that you produce evergreen products in your online business. I think this is perhaps one of the most painful and time-sucking lessons I have had to learn about this method of income generation.

Scalability & repurposing content

One of the most powerful aspects of digital product creation is in its ability to be scaled. This is a magical thing and can make you multiple times your basic income with very little work.

Let's take this book as an example. I write the book, it takes up, say, 100 hours of my time. Once the book is written, I release it as an ebook and a paperback; that's one book, two immediate profit lines, both as a consequence of repurposing existing content.

Next, I produce an audiobook and a workbook to accompany it. The audiobook doesn't require me to write anything new, the workbook is built around extracts from the main text.

Having created those four products, I can then sell them in the UK, the US, Australia, New Zealand, Iceland – anywhere in the world. My Kobo dashboard tells me I sell in 113 countries; I do that from a desk in my house. So, take that number as a benchmark – we have four products in 113 countries, that's 452 selling opportunities. I might add a training course to accompany the book and, perhaps more expensive 1-1 consultancy. As the number of products grows, so we multiply by the number of territories we can sell in, and the sales opportunities rapidly increase. Yes, all this grows from just one product.

The scalability potential of a digital product business is eye-watering; do the work once, sell it multiple times, in multiple territories, over multiple years.

The potential is incredible, and it all comes from your laptop and a couple of downloads onto your hard drive. I hope that by now your eyes are popping out on stalks like a TV cartoon character. This way of making money is exciting and it's no further away from you than the gap between your fingertips and your computer keyboard.

Key points:

- Creating and selling your own products is the perfect business. There's no stock, no staff, no premises and it's high profit.
- This is the ideal antidote to insecure employment and zero-hours contracts. You can be your own boss with only a laptop and basic software needed.
- Anybody can do this, and it doesn't matter if you're new to business or if you've already been in business for many years.

2

MY PRODUCT CREATION EXPERIENCE

Product creation is something that I fell into quite soon in my online marketing work. However, my own journey had a few iterations before I finally figured out my path forward. When I started online work, my strategy was to create an information website, one which Google loved due to its well-crafted content and consistent, topic-related keywords. This was in 2008 before I'd even discovered blogging, writing books and podcasting. If you look for the website web-work-at-home.com, you'll still be able to take a look at the archived version in the Wayback Machine. The service I used to make that site was SiteBuildIt, a service which offered a number of customisable PDF guides made available to customers to help them spread the word about SBI. By the way, a PDF is an electronic file which allows you to distribute and share highly formatted books, leaflets, brochures and presentations over email, for download and printing on a PC.

It was seeing these information-packed guides that first gave me the idea of sharing information in a similar manner, only authored by me instead of a third party. I wrote several of these books, creating them in Word documents, saving them as PDF files and selling and sharing them online. Here's a list of those literary classics:

- ClickBank Critical: How to Revive Your Inactive ClickBank Account
- Sales Funnel Success: How to Create Your Own Cash Siphoning System
- JV Giveaway Coach: How to Take Part in Your First JV Giveaway Event
- 25 Expert Tips to Boost Your Internet Marketing Business
- 10 Tips to Instantly Improve Your Performance in Giveaway Events

You can take a look at the covers for those books on the accompanying website for this book, Create-Digital-Products.com. Don't worry if you haven't got a clue what the topics are about, they were just niche elements of internet marketing which interested me.

From this amateur and humble start, I developed and built upon those first five products and went on to generate six-figure sales in massive online launches. I then repeated it all over again with fiction and non-fiction, though I'm still working on the six-figure bit with those. You wouldn't want me to give you unrealistic expectations now, would you?

So how did five DIY ebooks lead to six-figure sales? Read on, I'm happy to share my digital products journey in the hope it will inspire you to do the same.

Selling PDF ebooks

I used two strategies to get my online business going with these PDF guides. This was how it was done back in 2008/2009 by the way; even though the Kindle had been launched in 2007, it wasn't mainstream at that time. I sold the PDF guides, using a PayPal account, and I gave them away, in exchange for an email address. This is pretty well your digital product strategy rolled into one sentence. Your mantra should be:

Create digital products, then sell them for cash or give them away in exchange for an email address.

I'll explain why giving away digital products in exchange for an email address is a good idea later in the book. But it really was as simple as that. I sold digital books, which had no physical form, and every dollar which arrived in my PayPal account was sheer profit. I built up a list of email addresses in exchange for high-value freebies, then attempted to sell other products to those people because having their email address meant that I could send them subsequent offers.

Lesson learned: *Digital books are easy to make and, if they're packed with great information, customers are happy to buy them at decent prices.*

Training videos

I'm fortunate enough to have spent my life in the communications industry, both as a teacher and a broadcaster, so speaking into a microphone and showing people how to do stuff always came naturally to me. Having tumbled into the internet marketing rabbit hole, I discovered that many marketers were recording and selling their own how-to videos and decided to give it a go. Fortunately, I found this process very straightforward, so jumped in at the deep end. The first thing I did was to create how-to videos based on my PDF books and their related topics. I also recorded interviews with online marketers and sold the audio. With more media options, things were really beginning to pick up. I'd started to earn hundreds of dollars rather than just tens of dollars and I began to realise that this stuff worked.

Lesson learned: *Digital video and audio products have a high perceived value and can be sold at higher prices than digital books.*

Digital product launches

As I became more and more immersed in internet marketing, I began to pay for mentorship from people who were doing much better than me. I also started building up a more substantial product in preparation for a big launch, using the most popular platform at the time: ClickBank. I was beginning to meet marketers who were making thousands of dollars from massive online launches and I wanted a piece of that action.

I became friendly with a UK marketer, who I'll refer to as FC from now on. FC liked my fledgling product so much, he agreed to partner with me to bring it to market. In return, we would share the profits 50:50. At the time, FC was one of the biggest internet marketers in the ClickBank marketplace. He knew all the big guys and he had several six-figure launches behind him. I was learning from the best.

FC coached me through developing and improving my product and helped me to present it in a much more 'salesy' way. We spent $10,000 just getting a much sought-after copywriter to write the text for our sales page and our graphics cost us a fair bit too. I couldn't believe the money we were spending, I thought we'd go broke.

When it came to the launch, FC had partnered up with all the big hitters in the industry. They sent out emails promoting the product – called *Auto Cash Funnel* – and it sent us to number three in the ClickBank charts, generating six-figure sales in a matter of weeks. Believe me, there's nothing like the excitement of seeing sales rolling in by the minute, with customers falling over themselves to lay their hands on a product which you can't even hold.

FC and I went on to work on several six-figure launches together and had a very enjoyable online partnership. I learned so much from him and will be forever grateful for the skills and techniques which he taught me, information which I will be sharing with you in this book.

Lesson learned: *It's not about the product, it's about marketing. The product has to be of a good standard, but it won't sell without great marketing.*

Webinars

One of the strategies which internet marketers were using at the time was to hold webinars with partners, then halve the profits from any sales that were made. As part of our launch, FC and I had generated a very substantial list of email addresses, so we teamed up with one of FC's contacts and ran a webinar promoting his product.

At the time, I was spending a month in Spain with my

family, paid for from the proceeds of the ClickBank launch we'd just run. I wasn't even able to attend that webinar because we had such terrible broadband in the villa that we were renting, so I woke up to find that we'd made another six figures from that webinar while I was sleeping.

Now, in the interests of transparency, I have to tell you that FC and I went 50:50 with the marketer on the sales proceeds but we then went 60:40 on our cut because FC had a bigger list of emails to market to than I did. So, I pocketed £5000 for that night, and I was asleep at the time.

I'm not telling you this to boast or show off, I want you to see the magic of this process. We weren't even selling our own product; we were leveraging the success of an earlier product launch to generate more sales and greater impetus. We used another technique to generate another $10,000 from somebody else's product elsewhere in that project, by acting as affiliates, but I'll say more about that later on.

Lesson learned: *Webinars add huge value to anything. They allow sellers to connect with customers all over the world and are incredible sales machines.*

Membership sites

The next thing FC and I launched was a membership website. This is a wonderful thing to get into if you're a digital product creator, and we sweated the technique to its full potential.

First of all, we set up another product launch for a twelve-week training programme. This was called the 7-Figure Success Formula. Now, I know these titles sound extremely salesy – and they are – and that is one of the reasons I decided to pivot from this internet marketing arena and move into writing books. However, I'll say more about that later; there's a lot we should learn from the internet marketing industry.

FC and I got paid to deliver this training live, over twelve weeks, presenting information-packed webinars to our customers. I recorded those webinars, edited and repackaged them, then added them to a membership website so that it was available to that first batch of customers.

Then we sold it all over again, this time marketing exactly the same information to a different audience, without having to turn up to present the live training. Instead, they logged into the membership website that I'd already created for the customers who'd paid us the first time round. I repackaged and resold that training in several ways over the next couple of years; it was twelve live training events which were very well leveraged.

I hope that by now you're getting pretty excited about how this digital product creation and sales process is shaping up.

Lesson learned: *Membership sites are an excellent way of repurposing digital content and creating an ongoing, monthly recurring income.*

WordPress plugins

Before FC and I worked together on my own product launch, I helped him on one of his own product launches, this time in a very profitable WordPress plugin niche.

WordPress is the tool used by millions of businesses and individuals to create their websites, and its functionality is increased by plugins, many of which are free, others which are paid for.

FC had paid for a special plugin to be developed and he had built a big product launch around this item. It sold by the bucketload and he made a lot of money from that product.

Now, when you get into creating and selling WordPress plugins, they can be profitable, but you do need to bear in mind development and maintenance costs. A WordPress plugin is essentially a zip file which you can sell for a couple of hundred dollars a time if it has sufficient functionality and you're good at marketing.

For a short period, I went on to work with another big internet marketer to manage the development of a WordPress plugin. I learned a lot of lessons from this experience, all of them valuable. The marketing exercise was the same I'd executed with FC several times, but the plugin experience was unique.

Although WordPress plugins can be very profitable, and they follow exactly the same principles as any other digital product when it comes to selling them and making money from them, this was my first experience of getting my fingers burned. The problem with plugins is that they break, customers have problems installing and using them and, as WordPress updates, it forces plugin developers to update too. This was my first experience of a digital platform that I didn't want to get involved in; I'll explain more as we progress through the book.

Lesson learned: *WordPress plugins can be very lucrative, but they have a high degree of development hassle, lots of customer issues and require an ongoing commitment in terms of support and maintenance.*

Creating software

After a time in internet marketing, I grew tired of the salesy nature of the business. I was keen to provide great value to customers and I was also convinced by the monthly recurring income model. I wanted to create something that customers loved and needed, and which they would pay me for every month. In succeeding in this aim, I learned a final, punishing lesson about creating and selling digital products.

This product was called Fast Fan Pages and it was built in the very early days of Facebook. In the good old days of Facebook, before you had to pay for advertising to derive any benefit from the platform, it was a marketer's paradise.

Let's be clear about this, I have no ability to build software, however, I do know how to manage a project. So, I commissioned a highly talented coding expert who built a superb piece of software for me. We never met in person, but this gentleman was amazing, his coding work incredible.

I launched the software using all the skills I'd gathered to that date, supported by training videos, PDF guides, launch and how-to webinars, the lot. It did reasonably well too, and over time I repackaged it in many formats, using the core software to package several other products, a couple of which scraped six-figure launches.

However, just like the WordPress plugins, the software required ongoing maintenance and was intensive in the support it required. The software required Facebook login but got messed up when a user had more than one Facebook account. That is and always has been against Facebook's terms and conditions but running the Fast Fan Pages helpdesk taught me how many people completely ignored that rule.

I also learned a very important lesson from that software experience; always take great care when your product relies on a third-party service. One day, I woke up to find that – without warning – Facebook had changed a technical specification without bothering to mention it to people like me who made software products. I had to pay for expensive work to quickly fix the software so that it worked properly. Lucky for me I was working with a superb coder, but it taught me that Facebook can be a cruel master.

Over time, Facebook changed business pages beyond recognition, meaning that my product became obsolete. When I spotted that coming on the horizon, I took the steps required to run that business down. It was profitable for a short time but flawed as a concept.

<u>Lesson learned</u>: *Never rely on a third-party platform for your income; they can annihilate your business in an instant. Do use talented freelancers to do the things you cannot do yourself.*

Writing & selling books 21st-century style

After I wound down this software product, I spent a little time in the product creation wilderness. I had experienced amazing sales and great success, but I had also learned some hard lessons along the way.

When I reflected on my position, I was able to make a list of the pros and cons of product creation:

- Digital books, video training programmes and expert interview audios are easy to produce, easy to sell and have a high perceived value. They also have minimal customer support requirements.

- Software products can be highly profitable, but they take an entirely different level of commitment. They are also heavily support dependent.
- Building a business that depends entirely upon a third-party service is like building a business on quicksand.
- Using freelancers who have skills that I do not possess is an excellent strategy for getting difficult things done.
- Although the quality of the product is always important, it's the marketing of that product that is most crucial. You won't be able to sell a great product with bad marketing, but you will be able to sell a bad product with great marketing. I wanted to sell great products with great marketing.

This is where I stumbled into writing books. I'd always written since the age of ten years old. I'd even had some books banned by Amazon in the early days of the Kindle Gold Rush, when I'd tried an experiment with Private Label Rights (PLR) material only to get my knuckles rapped. More about PLR later.

I'd already written five PDF books of my own and had some success with those. I had also just written my first science fiction book while I was at a loose end, trying to figure out what to do next. Then, as if by magic, all the pieces fell into place for me; I would become a writer and build a sales system around my books. And I would focus, with laser precision, on creating products which didn't rely entirely on one platform, which didn't date as fast as internet marketing products did and which would create a residual income for me which my family could benefit from 70 years after my death, under present UK copyright law. This new strategy would allow me to harness all those lessons learned and turn them into a residual income-generating, high-power marketing machine.

That's where you find me now, at the time of writing this book. It's a lot slower following this strategy as books take some time to write, but on the day I'm writing these words, here are my numbers after four years:

- Over 4.5 million pages read on Amazon (I get paid for each page)
- Over 37 thousand books sold
- Over 236,000 books given away (these translate to purchases and pages read)

Although writing fiction is definitely not for everyone, it's my non-fiction strategy that this book will focus on primarily. In the chapters that follow I will tell you how to create and sell the most profitable information products and to market them in a way that will help you to squeeze out every available dollar from each transaction.

This stuff works. As I write this, I've just enjoyed my most lucrative author sales month ever. I have generated over $12,000 of digital sales from a 0.99 boxset which just sold more than 15,000 copies and accrued well over 1.8 million page reads, all of which I get paid for. That's incredible, you can't even hold my book to read it, yet it's made all that money in just one month. I'm not even a bestselling author, I'm a regular guy writing half-decent books but marketing them effectively. And that cash was generated from work I did over the past three years, using the same marketing principles I learned from FC. And I did it in the midst of an international pandemic, which has seen millions of people losing their jobs, income and security, selling something that doesn't even exist in the physical world.

This is definitely not a book that's only for authors. I'll be guiding you through the entire catalogue of profit-making principles that I deployed to create all these successful launches. You can use these techniques in any field, whatever your job or area of expertise, it works for everybody if you apply what I'm about to tell.

Ready to get started? Let's get stuck in.

Key points:

- Focus on PDF, video and audio products, they're simpler to produce and come with very few problems.
- Avoid software and WordPress plugins unless you're happy to commit to heavier customer support and ongoing development costs.
- Beware relying on third-party platforms; if they change something without warning it makes you very vulnerable.

3

DIGITAL FORMATS & TERMINOLOGY

It's important to know which file formats to use before you launch on your product creation career. Many of these formats you will be familiar with already, but it's worth me saying a few words about each so that you understand why I prefer these formats above any other options.

Of course, it's up to you what you settle on finally, but I'll give you my two cents here so you're aware of the thinking behind each strategy.

The other point I have to make is that I'm a PC, not an Apple user. I have made Apple suggestions as I've gone along, and most of the tools I use offer Apple options anyway.

PDF products

Here's a piece of information you can read then immediately forget. PDF stands for Portable Document Format. You'll never need that information ever again. I had to look that up, by the way, it's so inconsequential to my use of this file format.

When you create and sell digital products, the PDF file needs to become your friend. It's a much more effective way for you to pass on text files because it locks fonts and images into the file. If you share text documents as Word files, you run into all sorts of issues such as which version of Word the reader is using and if your content displays the way you want it to.

The other advantage of a PDF file is that you can send out a single file and it can be read on a Mac or a PC, without having to create a special version.

PDF files can be made from a Word document (I'll mention OpenOffice later in the book) by clicking on **File**, selecting **Save a Copy**, then clicking on **PDF** in the drop-down menu.

That might be a little different in older versions of Word, but doesn't that just illustrate my point that it's best to use PDF files so that everybody has the same experience?

Use PDF files when customers are receiving content via email or downloading from a website. They can be any length you want, with or without images and with or without weblinks. They're suitable for use with transcriptions, illustrated how-to guides to accompany videos, worksheets and activity pages as well as long-form books. Generally, if a PDF is longer than ten thousand words, I'd consider making it into a book, delivered via PDF, MOBI or EPUB.

Audio products (MP3, WAV & M4A)

There's a lot more choice when it comes to creating audio files. I think it's fair to say that most people will have heard of MP3 files and WAV files for audio recordings.

In simple terms, WAV files are larger and higher quality

than MP3 files, which compress the audio more to make the file size smaller. Why does that matter? If you download WAV files onto your smartphone, you'll soon run out of space, whereas you'll squeeze a lot more MP3 files into the same storage allocation.

These files were created by the Moving Pictures Expert Group – hence the MPEG – and are abbreviated from MPEG-3. They're very commonly used and are the safest format to use for audio products.

WAV is short for Waveform and because they are lossless and uncompressed, they lose no quality from the original recording. MP3 files are known as 'lossy' because they do the opposite.

Without making your eyes glaze over, for the purposes of digital product creation, MP3 files are smaller and easier to deliver; WAV files are too big and our customers won't thank us for filling up their hard drives with them.

Just to confuse you a little more, you may come across the newer M4A audio file format. I would advise sticking with MP3 files for now, it will make things a lost easier from a customer familiarity point of view.

Audio files can be used for interviews, reading out the content of PDF files, commentary and how-to guides. No more than an hour is best if bundled as part of a product – aim for 30-60 minutes. If you're recording podcasts, it doesn't matter so long as the content is interesting, on topic and relevant. Audiobook content length is divided into chapters, with each chapter being recorded into a different file.

Video products (MP4)

I think it's fair to say that the MP4 file format is most common for recording video, but if you're a Mac user, you're more likely to use MOV files.

MP4 is short for MPEG-4, a video file format which is highly versatile for digital product creation use. It can store subtitles, audio and still images as well as being compressed, which means it does all that without creating a massive file.

The MOV file is Apple's equivalent of this, and along with MP4 video files, can be easily uploaded to YouTube without any problems.

I would suggest steering clear of AVI, FLV or FLV video file formats, because they're not the most commonly used and you're more likely to run into compatibility issues with them.

Sticking my neck out here, and at the risk of offending Mac users, I'd suggest keeping to MP4 for the sake of simplicity.

Video how-to guides should be a maximum of 30 minutes in duration for the sake of keeping our attention, but a sustained presentation on a particular topic – in a webinar-style teaching format – can be an hour to 90 minutes.

Digital book products (MOBI & EPUB)

It's important not to confuse the reasons why we would use PDF files instead of MOBI and EPUB files. The latter are file types which allow people with e-readers to access files and to consume them as if they were a book.

The book you are reading now has been processed as

both MOBI and EPUB files, but it is not available as a PDF file. That's because it is a book rather than a document or a guide and is therefore best consumed on a device which replicates that reader experience. Also, MOBI and EPUB files have better functionality.

A MOBI file is the name given to a Mobipocket ebook file which is used for storing digital books on mobile devices with low bandwidth – that means the file sizes are smaller than PDFs.

They also support bookmarking, notes and so on, but they're not good for illustration-heavy documents, which PDFs most certainly are.

EPUB is short for electronic publication and this file type allows you to read books on smartphones, tablets, computers and tablets. It's a freely available standard format and is more widely available than any other ebook reading format.

When it comes to MOBI and EPUB files, think Betamax and VHS video formats, but in this case, they both won.

Web-based products

I'm not going to beat around the bush here. If you're setting up a website for digital product sales, use WordPress.

I know that guy in the IT department said Drupal is better quality code. I also know your best pal who has made their own hobby website used Wix and it was free and works fine. I don't care. I've been doing this for a long time, and I can tell you that the only product that is fit for purpose for digital product creators and sellers is WordPress.

Put simply, if there's something you want to do with WordPress you will be able to do it. 'But what about Shopify?' I hear you cry. No! Use WordPress. 'Squarespace?' Enough already. No, no, no, use WordPress. When you're setting up a digital content-based business, WordPress will be able to cope with anything you throw at it. It is a highly supported website creation tool, which means there's loads of cool stuff you can use – often for free – which will solve pretty well any product delivery issues you have.

It's also crucially important to own your own web presence. By all means, set up shops on Shopify or Etsy, but always consider your own WordPress sites as the 'mother ship' of your business, the place where you can sell directly to customers. You'll get a good SEO – search engine optimization – boost for images and listings in these sites, but please remember the sad tale of building my Facebook software on a third-party platform. If you only use a third-party service to deliver your digital products, you're vulnerable to them locking you out, not paying you, increasing their fees and undermining your profitability or going out of business themselves.

In my internet marketing career, I have personally met marketers who used to sell digital products on eBay. Several years ago now, eBay decided to cease selling digital products and these vendors lost lucrative businesses overnight.

In addition, WordPress will make it easy for you to deliver your digital products via various payment processors; it really is the most versatile way of setting up your business.

I'm not going to explore WordPress in great detail in this book, but I will take you directly to the source of the well. To set up a WordPress website for a reasonable price and without overcomplicating the process, use SiteGround's WordPress hosting service. It's reasonably priced, has everything you need and offers great support. I'm not even going to suggest any alternatives: SiteGround is the source of the well.

The free and paid plugins that WordPress makes available to you will enable you to securely sell and deliver your digital products as well as building lucrative membership services around them. And if running a WordPress site seems too much for you, there are plenty of people who will maintain it for a small monthly fee, if your budget allows.

Software products

As I've already explained, this book is not going to deal with software products, other than mentioning them where relevant.

However, it's worth me mentioning a software product basic in this section if you do pursue that route. Deliver your software service as a cloud-based product, downloadable EXE (executable) files are old-fashioned and will get flagged by antivirus software time and time again.

Software is best delivered as a SAAS product – Software as a Service – and I strongly recommend that you never sell software as a one-time payment. Remember, it takes constant updating and maintenance, you must price that into your income model. SAAS products have recurring payments built-in, users can be denied access if they stop paying and you get the ongoing income you need to support and grow your service.

Sell a one-time download and you're opening yourself up to a world of customer service grief.

SAAS products come with what's known as the *pain of disconnect* – that is, it's often easier to keep using them than it is to cancel your subscription or move to a new product.

PLR: Private Label Rights

This is not a term that's widely known outside internet marketing circles, but it is a concept which can be a source of additional profit for product creators.

In the early days of my online career, I used to sell PLR versions of those first PDF ebooks that I created. In simple terms, it means that for an additional fee, you make your products available with additional usage rights for the buyer. They, in turn, can adapt the products and claim them as their own; it's a little bit like a licensing premium, but without all the legal hassles.

Here are some of the selling options available:

- Basic Resale Rights – you have the right to sell the product to others and keep 100 per cent of the profits. You do not need to pay royalties per sale. The person to whom you sell the product does not have the right to resell the product to others.
- Master Resale Rights – you have the right to sell the product to others and keep 100 per cent of the profits. You do not need to pay royalties per sale. You can also sell the Basic Resale Rights to others so that person has the right to also sell the product to others.

This is an excellent way of creating a digital product and then generating income from it time after time. Take the example of a PDF guide you might produce for a legal firm, outlining the key legal terms that customers need to use. You could sell that product directly to legal firms, with your name on it as the author. You could also sell it with Basic

Resale Rights so that they can brand it and claim it as their own guide. They'd pay extra for that, of course. It's a bit like a white-label deal, only the simple licence is usually supplied with the product and lawyers are not involved. It's a simple, dynamic way to make cash from your product. And, for an even higher fee, if they really liked it, you could sell them the rights to pass it onto their own industry colleagues so that they, in turn, could brand it too.

The concept is that we do the work once with digital products then repackage and sell them many times. It's the same amount of work but with more profit built-in by using different sales and marketing strategies.

Key points:

- Use MP3 for audio, MP4 for video and PDF for test files unless your product is a conventional book format where MOBI or EPUB will be used.
- However tempting, do not be distracted from using WordPress as your main website.
- Don't even think about downloadable software if you pursue that route; become familiar with SAAS.

4

ESSENTIAL TOOLS FOR DIGITAL PRODUCT CREATION

As well as needing to know the basic file types that we'll use to get your digital product creation career underway, it's also important to assemble the correct items in your toolkit. We don't need much to be able to set up this lucrative business, but you will need to assemble some essential kit.

I've been creating digital products for over a decade now, so I have a good idea what makes life easy and what will get in the way. Here are some common and recommended options, along with my thoughts about them.

Word

This is probably the most common word processing tool and it's hard in this modern day and age not to have encountered it at some stage in your life in education or at work. I view it as a necessary evil in that it's bloated software which often doesn't behave and is far more complicated than it needs to be. It also has a recurring price tag attached to it which puts off many users.

Unfortunately, in spite of all its issues, Word does the

job, so if you own it already – and I do, through gritted teeth – make it a part of your toolkit. It's also ready for Mac or PC use.

OpenOffice

If the cost of Word is prohibitive to you, or if you simply dislike it, there is a free alternative available to you. It's an Open Source software called OpenOffice which gives you access to a lookalike version of the key Microsoft software suite: Word, Excel and PowerPoint.

There's nothing at all wrong with OpenOffice and it's what I used in the early days of my digital product business. It's easy to make the switch from Microsoft too, so you'll have no problem finding your way around.

OpenOffice is backwards and forwards compatible, which means that you can create files which open on Word and you can also open documents which were created in Word. So, it gives you no disadvantages at all, and it is genuinely free, with no lives to be signed away and no adverts.

OpenOffice also makes versions for PCs and Macs.

Google Drive

I was a very early adopter of Google's original Drive service, which provides a cloud-based alternative to the Microsoft Office suite.

Google Docs replaces Word, Google Sheets replaces Excel and Google Slides replaces PowerPoint. In my opinion, these services are what Microsoft's products should be like. They're stripped-down, removing all the bloat, but retaining the key features. There's also a little-known service tucked away in there called Google Forms which is an excellent, free survey tool, every bit as good as Survey Monkey but without its prohibitive price tag.

Google Drive is mainly browser-based, but you can set it up so that it synchronises with your hard drive. In this scenario, it works with both PCs and Macs.

Canva

When I started my digital product creation business, the only real option for creating graphics was to use Photoshop Elements. The full software was expensive and bloated for professional use, whereas the simpler Elements option made life a lot easier.

Fast forward several years and there's very little point using any other product but Canva these days. It removes all requirements for technical knowledge, allowing you to make images for your digital products, ebook covers, social media posts, YouTube videos, logos, CD covers – you name it, you can make it, with templates aplenty.

In addition, Canva takes care of sourcing images and graphics and they're all great quality and correctly licensed so you won't run into any copyright issues.

Canva is browser-based, so you can use it on PCs and Macs.

Camtasia

If you intend to create videos as part of your digital product business – and I strongly recommend that you do – you're going to need a screen recording software. This is software which records what's on your PC screen, meaning that you can turn a slides presentation or a PC-based demonstration into a paid-for training product. This software also allows you to record your audio commentary.

Over a decade ago, when I started creating my first digital products, I made the decision to purchase Camtasia, a desktop-based software which I have happily used ever since. Camtasia is pricey but I love it and use it virtually every day. However, I realise that at over £200, this definitely won't be for everybody, so I've recommended a free alternative below.

Camtasia is my preferred service and the one that I use in my own business, so it's right that I mention it here. By the way, you can – and therefore should – download a free trial to take it out for a spin.

Screencast-O-Matic

This free and low-cost alternative to Camtasia has been around for years, so it's tried and tested. In fact, this is what I started using when I first began recording training videos for my internet marketing launches. It's come a long way since those days and should not be regarded as second-best; it does everything that Camtasia does.

The reason I opted for Camtasia is that I prefer the editing flexibility; Screencast-O-Matic has always been quite restricted in that area. If you're on a budget or you just want to get the hang of screen recording first, this service is a great place to get started.

Vellum

If you intend to produce professional guides in MOBI, EPUB or PDF formats as a part of your digital business, Vellum is the best software to enable you to do this. This option wasn't available when I was doing my internet marketing launches, but I would have used it to format my how-to guides in PDF format as they would have looked more professional than my Word-to-PDF versions.

If you're creating non-fiction content too, Vellum will allow you to easily output the files that Amazon, Google Books, Apple Books, Kobo, and Barnes & Noble require. For the purposes of this book, I'm only going to consider the use of MOBI and EPUB files in order to create short pre-sales guides to encourage prospects and customers into our sales system, to move them across to training services or membership sites. To get chapter and verse on how to write a fiction book, please check out my book The 5-Figure Fiction Formula.

Vellum is made to be used on Macs, but if you use the MacinCloud software, you'll be able to access it on a PC too.

Key points:

- Always start with free software or free trials if you can, don't be in a rush to spend money.
- Although I prefer Google Docs for text file creation, OpenOffice and Word are perfectly good too, though more complicated.
- My preferred screen recording software is Camtasia, but Screencast-O-Matic is an excellent, free and paid substitute.

5

DIGITAL PRODUCT CREATION TIPS & TECHNIQUES

Now that we've established the tools of the trade, it's time to dig a little deeper into the types of product that can be created. Because I've launched so many different products over a period of more than a decade, I also want to share the things I learned along the way, to save you from hitting the same potholes in the road.

Websites & membership sites

I've now lost count of how many times I have installed WordPress. It's been my go-to website creation tool for many years now, longer than I have been creating digital products. Without turning this book into a 'how to install WordPress' guide, let me give you the pointers that you need to fast track this process:

- Use SiteGround's WordPress hosting.
- Once you have an account, make for the cPanel area.

- Head for the WordPress installer and follow the simple prompts.
- That's it! You have a WordPress website, no geekery required.

The trick to installing WordPress is not to overcomplicate it. And once installed, it's easy to use and adapt to your purposes.

You're going to use WordPress a lot on your product creation journey and it is more than capable of coping with anything you care to throw at it. Its main purpose is for product sales and content delivery; in simple terms, you need to create a sales page and then, having sold your item, you need a place to send your customer so that they can download it.

To give you a sense of how useful WordPress can be, here is a shortlist of some of my own product launches and how WordPress was deployed in each situation:

- 7 Figure Success Formula – a twelve-week programme of live training which was then repackaged as a membership website. WordPress managed the sales page, the live webinar replay resource pages and the entire membership site element of the repackaged training product.
- Affiliate Fan Pages – this was the training and delivery website used to resell a version of my Facebook software to an internet marketing audience. The original product was called Fast Fan Pages and was aimed at small business owners. However, using the same software delivery mechanism, the software was 'reimagined' as an

automated sales system for internet marketers and sold on different platforms where the selling style was very different. WordPress was used to deliver sales pages, training and product downloads.

- PaulTeague.net – this appears to be a simple author website, but it is in fact a flexible sales engine. I use it to promote and sell my fiction books via Amazon or – if I have listed my books wide – via Google, Barnes & Noble, Apple Books and Kobo. I am also able to sell my non-fiction books directly to the customer using Payhip, which I'll be saying more about later. In addition, I use this WordPress website to collect emails from people who are browsing there and I use special web code in the background to enable me to retarget them on Facebook and Google – and yes, I will be saying more about that technique too when we dig into marketing strategies.

In short, WordPress makes all this easy and allows me to create on-demand marketing machines. There's nothing quite like it available anywhere else.

PDF guides

My first PDF guides were where I cut my teeth learning how to create and sell digital products. I'll be honest, I only knew the rudimentary elements of using Word at the time and, when I left the BBC to start up on my own, I didn't want to shell out for a Microsoft Word licence, so used OpenOffice instead.

I made heavy use of PDF guides when I got started and I still use them now as an author. These days I produce them in a different way, but they're still just as handy as they were more than a decade ago. PDFs are such a simple way of creating and sharing great information, they have to be a core part of your digital product armoury.

Here's how I have used them in the past:

- My first PDF books were illustrated how-to guides aimed at newbie internet marketers. They were a mixture of text, images and weblinks. The weblinks were to affiliate products. If the reader clicked and went on to buy those products, I would take a commission of 50% on average. I would most often give these books away for free because I made my money from those affiliate products. I've reserved an entire chapter for affiliate marketing, by the way.
- In the past 24 hours, I have listed one of my non-fiction books for sale via Payhip so that I can sell directly to customers and retain more profit. In order to deliver my book securely to the customer, I use a delivery service called BookFunnel, which can also be used to deliver free book samples by the way. Instead of sending the customer directly to a PDF file, the process is made more secure by using BookFunnel to restrict that download access. Rather than delivering the book in Payhip after I make the sale, I have a PDF document which explains to the customer how they will receive their purchase, how to access it and where to go for support. I have sold many books using this method and never had a customer request more support because it has made the process so clear.

- When I was selling Fast Fan Pages, my Facebook software service, I used PDF documents to create readable versions of my how-to videos, incorporating text and screenshots. Customers like to learn in different ways, some hate having to rely on videos, so ready-made, illustrated notes help to build the value of what you're selling, as well as the utility.

Even as an author, nowadays publishing my books in MOBI and EPUB format, I still have plenty of uses for PDF files. I'd actually go so far as to describe them as the most important tool in your digital product creation toolkit.

Video training

I must have produced hundreds of hours of video training in my product creation career. It's a lot easier than it used to be too; these days you can upload it all to YouTube and let them take the strain of hosting costs. You can run up a bill very quickly if you pay for video hosting yourself.

I continue to use video regularly in my business; it's such a handy tool and so easy to deploy now we've moved out of the dark ages of dial-up internet and RealPlayer files, which is the old technology used to deliver BBC streams and videos just after the turn of the century. Here's how I have used videos in my digital product creation work:

- For creating sales promotion videos using Camtasia, stock images and a PowerPoint presentation. The biggest internet launch I was ever involved in – Auto Cash Funnel – hit six figures in sales as a result of the sales videos I recorded using this technique. I went on to record the sales videos for Auto Cash Funnel, Fast Fan Pages, 7-Figure Success Formula and many more products using this technique.

- I've lost count of the number of how-to videos created in my internet marketing career, with the videos being delivered initially on old-fashioned HTML web pages, then later using WordPress. As well as using them for lucrative internet marketing launches like Instant Profit Pages and Property Millionaire Maker (yes, they really were two of the products I worked on – titles like that make products sell), I also used them as an author in my Patreon account, where subscribers paid to support my work, rather than paying directly for the videos.

- One of the elements of creating and selling digital products which I like least is providing customer support. For this reason, I have dedicated an entire chapter to the topic later on. However, screen share videos are an excellent way of showing people what to do if they're simply not getting it; a picture paints a thousand words as the saying goes. In the past week I have used this technique on my author Facebook page to show potential readers who don't own a Kindle device how to access my books using the free Kindle reader app on their computer, laptop or mobile phone, thus resulting in more sales.

Along with PDF files, videos are a format that you really need to master. As a man who spent almost two decades behind a radio microphone, I don't like to appear on camera, so you can take some solace in the knowledge that the majority of the videos that I made have allowed me to remain hidden. Here are the video formats you can use, I have deployed all of these in my digital marketing career:

- PowerPoint presentations with voice-only commentary. Also, the option of adding a webcam feed to this content.
- Screen share videos where you give voice commentary as you show how to do something on your computer screen. Also, the option of adding a webcam feed to this content.
- Directly to a webcam – where you sit at your PC and speak directly into the camera, with your image taking up the full screen.
- Directly to camera – where you're filmed as if a TV presenter. This is the technique we used for Property Millionaire Maker, where the product host guided viewers around his properties whilst discussing teaching points.

The great thing about video is that it has a high perceived value and can be sold at a variety of price points. Forget corporate standards of production too. See if you can find Zoella's first-ever video on her YouTube channel; how's that for low production values? How would you like Zoella's bank balance? Nuff said!

Audio downloads

I've made frequent use of audio as part of my digital content strategy and I guess you'd expect that from somebody who comes from a radio background. Please don't neglect audio;

think how big Amazon's Audible service is. Just take a look at any bus or train and see how many of your potential customers are using earbuds – they could be consuming your content.

Here's how I have made money from audio files:

- Recording interviews with internet marketing success stories, then selling the audio files and transcriptions as part of a masterclass product.
- Running a podcast – in this scenario, the interviews and associated web pages created SEO-friendly content which drives organic web traffic to those pages. By adding appropriate affiliate products to that website, it helps to generate income. In addition, I have used 'interview extras' as content in a paid Patreon website.
- Audio options in online training are a great way of value building. I mentioned earlier that PDF files to accompany videos help to build up the value of a product, well so too do audio files. In Camtasia, it takes a few seconds to strip the MP3 file out of a ready-to-go video.
- Creating audio versions of an ebook can help to generate more income from an existing asset i.e. a book that you've already written. Due to the production costs, if you pay for a narrator, I'd recommend avoiding this with your fiction works until you know there is sufficient demand. However, non-fiction, in particular, lends itself to being recorded by the author, in that it is already written in the way they speak and phrase sentences. In addition, readers will often buy a

non-fiction audiobook, find that there's lots of great content contained there, and then go out and buy the paperback too, so that they can easily refer back to it.
- Hint: BookFunnel allows you to upload and share audio files but there is a limit on file size.

Audio is the forgotten jewel in the crown of digital content creation. It's a breeze to create from videos that you have made already, so it makes sense to strip out MP3 to give an alternative for customers who prefer to learn in that way as well as building up huge value around the product you are selling.

Publishing ebooks

This is the main strategy I have used in my content creation business since 2014 and now is a good opportunity to point out why that is. There's an important lesson contained in these words, please take note.

The lesson I have learned in producing digital products is to avoid creating content which dates quickly. Always seek evergreen product creation opportunities, they remain active for much longer and give you a better bang for your buck. In supermarket terms, we need to think UHT milk, not fresh milk; think breadmaking mixes, not fresh loaves. The longer your products stick around without the need to be updated, the more profitable they become.

The reason I pivoted to writing books, and bear in mind that I still use all the techniques in this book alongside that work, is that fiction doesn't go stale and I can make income from it for my estate 70 years after my death. Think of the authors who have films and TV series made of their books years after publication. Game of Thrones is an excellent example of this. Digital products should be regarded as assets which can be sold and repackaged time and time again.

Here's a taste of my ebook projects:

- I write non-fiction as P. Teague and generate affiliate income around the products that I recommend. I intend to create audiobooks of my non-fiction titles at some point and may consider training courses and consultancy in future.
- I write psychological thrillers as Paul J. Teague. I sell these as standalone novels, but also write in series so that I can build up box sets which can be priced for extra profits. My most lucrative fiction promotion involved packaging twelve of my existing stories as a huge omnibus edition; it sold many thousands of copies.
- I write science fiction as Paul Teague. As well as deploying the same strategies as I do with my psychological thrillers, I also teamed up with another author who has strong connections with some big hitters in that genre. This has allowed me to access partners and readers which I wouldn't normally be able to access, hence enabling me to grow the audience for my solo projects and generate more income.

Writing fiction definitely isn't for everybody and I will focus primarily on non-fiction in this book because it so adeptly supports what we are doing with our other digital products. A non-fiction book often sits at the very beginning of a sales funnel, another term which you'll be familiar with by the end of this book.

Repurposing

In concluding this chapter, I want to introduce you to a key principle of product creation, that of repurposing your content. Many of the examples I have given you involve taking one format then recreating it in a different medium or bundling it with something that you produced already to sell at a higher price or to package in a newly-titled project.

Start thinking of all digital content as assets which can be packaged and sold in many different ways. When I'm teaching people about internet work, this is one of my favourite phrases:

Do the work once, profit from it many times.

Memorise and deploy that process, it will serve you very well in your life as a digital product creator. A great example of how I did this was with my Facebook software. That core service was repackaged and sold as Fast Fan Pages, Affiliate Fan Pages, Instant Profit Pages and Clixeo, the corporate and white label version. Do the work once, profit from it many times.

Key points:

- Think laterally when creating digital products – always ask yourself which product options you can offer as part of your product.

- Think long term and avoid creating products which will date quickly.
- Always consider how products could be bundled together or presented in a different way in order to increase the profitability of work you have already done.

6

BACKUP, STORAGE AND SIMPLE PRODUCT DELIVERY

During one of my early internet launches I discovered that my product was being given away for free on a Black Hat website. These websites share all sorts of cheats and unofficial access information, meaning that people can help themselves to your product without paying.

I challenged the owner of the site about this and received the nonchalant reply that my WordPress website was wide open, unprotected and that anybody could help themselves to that content if they knew where to look. That person did me a favour because I wasn't aware of that at the time.

Now, don't get me wrong, it wasn't like I lost thousands of pounds from this experience, but I did learn an important lesson: protect your products from being stolen. In this case, it was my bad. You can bet your life I put it right straight away. It's crucial to store and deliver your digital products securely.

It's not just theft that you have to worry about, you also need to pay some attention to how you store and organise your products so that you don't lose or delete them. I have every project I have ever created backed up on external hard drives and in cloud-based accounts. I've been very glad of that meticulous backup and storage particularly because I've been doing this for over a decade now. So here are some tips I've learned along the way.

Google Drive

Google Drive is one of my favourite tools and I've been using it for years. As I type the words to this very book, I am sharing this document with a team of listeners to my podcast who are reading it as I go along, and adding their feedback to help me improve the text. I have used it so heavily, I now have to pay an annual fee to Google because I have exceeded the free storage limits; believe me, that takes some doing.

Primarily, Google Drive should be used for the creation and storage of documents such as Word and PowerPoint. However, you can store pretty well anything else on it too. I've uploaded all sorts in the past.

Google Drive is a cloud-based system, but you can download a file which automatically synchronises everything you save onto your PC. You can also collaborate with partners in Google Drive and it will allow you to create secure sharing links too, which means you could actually use the service for a very simple product delivery system.

A simple click of the **Share** button will allow you to give access to other people by email address or by creating a public share link. In addition, you can restrict the files so that they cannot be downloaded or changed.

I would recommend Google Drive for storage, sharing and backup rather than product delivery, but it's perfectly fine for that purpose if you have a fairly simple product which is stored as a document.

Dropbox

This is a much more robust and versatile cloud storage system than Google Drive and I have my entire online life backed up in Dropbox. I was early to use cloud-based systems and in the olden days, they used to slow your computer down as they uploaded huge files. I don't know how Dropbox manages the technology, but you're barely aware of it uploading your files in the background.

The key difference between Dropbox and Google Drive is that Dropbox is specifically created as a full backup system and its pricing structure takes that into account. I back up everything to Dropbox.

As a prolific creator of content, I am particularly keen on Dropbox's online-only option, which stores everything in the cloud, but lets you 'pull it down' instantly when you need it on your hard drive. In effect, it creates a drive on your PC where you can see every one of your backed-up files, but they're not actually on your PC, they're sitting in the cloud. Believe me, when you've accrued over 10 years' worth of digital content, that provides instant relief for your computer.

Just like Google Drive, Dropbox can create access links to files and folders, meaning that you can use it for digital product delivery and collaboration.

OneDrive

If you subscribe to the Microsoft Office cloud-based version as I do, Microsoft gives you a huge amount of cloud storage as part of the deal. Their cloud-based system is called OneDrive and I've grown to love this more and more over the years, to the extent that it's in danger of becoming my favourite. Dropbox's simpler online-only feature just clinches the crown.

OneDrive offers more flexible share options, including sharing documents to social media and even allows you to generate HTML embed code to make a document available directly within a web page. That's a great option for hassle-free product delivery via your website.

As it is, I use OneDrive as a second source of full hard drive backups because I get it bundled in an existing purchase. I tried to switch off Dropbox recently because I felt like I was double-paying for one service, but I like that online-only function far too much to cut the cord on Dropbox.

WordPress/Web Storage

I'll be delving into WordPress in much greater detail later in the book because my official position on this matter is that you should use one of a variety of available plugins to securely store and deliver your content. This will spare you an experience like mine on a Black Hat website.

At this stage, where we're keeping things basic, I want you to understand that if you upload a Word or PDF file to WordPress, it is publicly visible by default if you know where to look for it. It's very tempting to upload all of your PDF files there because it's a very simple storage and sharing system, but it's not the cleverest way to do things.

Also, a WordPress page can be protected by a password, but that only limits access to the page itself, the link to the

PDF is still completely open to somebody with a bit of technical knowledge helping themselves.

For simple document access on a WordPress website, I recommend the PDF Embedder plugin by Lever Technology LLC. I used this to give course attendees access to slides for many years, where I didn't want those files distributed and shared beyond the course delegates.

Beyond this simple solution, you really need to be considering built-for-purpose membership plugins, and this is the best way to lock down content and specific areas of a website, with a variety of access options. I'll look at this topic in detail later in the book.

YouTube

Videos usually exist as MOV and MP3 files when you record and edit them, but for customers to access them securely, they really need to be hosted online. That means you'll need some form of membership site delivery so that those videos can't be shared or stolen.

Once again, I'll offer more robust solutions for this issue later in the book, but for now, there is a simple solution for this which keeps life simple.

I frequently run 1-1 consultation over Zoom with corporate clients and I record these and make the replays available afterwards. So as not to overcomplicate this matter, I take the recorded file from Zoom, remove the chit-chat at the beginning and the end of the session, then upload the file to YouTube.

YouTube offers three options for uploaded videos, the default being **Public.** However, you can also mark videos as **Unlisted** and this is the simplest way to be able to share a video with only the people who you wish to have access to it. It remains hidden from everybody else. You also have the option to mark a video as **Private**, which means it is for your eyes only.

This is a basic way of restricting access to video content, but it's one I use myself on a frequent basis. There's no point in overcomplicating matters if a simple solution is available.

BookFunnel

I use BookFunnel as a fiction and non-fiction author, and it wasn't available when I was doing my big internet marketing launch, or I would certainly have used it. Put simply, if you have MOBI, EPUB, PDF or MP3 files to deliver, you can bypass having to set up a WordPress website in order to promote and securely deliver these items. Book-Funnel comes with a modest price tag, but it is an effective digital product delivery system with all sorts of marketing extras baked in. It could actually be renamed 'ProductFunnel' and find an entirely new audience, it's that good.

BookFunnel allows you to create customised sales and landing pages (which collect email addresses) as well as download pages which restrict the number of downloads that can be made, and allow you to change a link if it gets shared online without your permission.

An additional feature is the option to give away codes for print versions of your books – on-demand printing is highly recommended in spite of this book being focused on digital products. You can use that for worksheets and checklists too.

BookFunnel links with several payment processors – PayPal, Selz, Payhip, Shopify and WooCommerce at the time of writing. It even manages fulfilment and support – that's a fabulous offering, believe me.

You can turn it into a marketing machine too, because not only does it integrate with email marketing services such as MailerLite, Mailchimp, ConvertKit and ActiveCampaign, it provides a marketplace so that you can team up with other product creators to promote your products. The BookFunnel team also provides all the customer support.

All in all I love BookFunnel; all they have to do is to add secure video access and they've created the perfect product delivery machine for beginners.

A word about security

Please be mindful of security matters when using cloud backup services. It goes without saying that your passwords should be secure and use lowercase and uppercase letters, numbers and special characters. I use LastPass for secure password storage; Dashlane and RoboForm are great alternatives.

However, if you're going to build a business, I would recommend you go further than this. Use a form of 2FA – two-factor authentication – as well. The most common way to do this is to set up mobile phone text codes.

I prefer to go one step even further than this, using an app-based authentication tool. The one you'll see most commonly is the Google Authenticator app which, in simple terms, generates personalised codes for you to use when logging in. Authy authenticator is a better option though because you can also access it on your computer which means that you're not locked out of your accounts if you ever lose your phone. At the time of writing, the Google Authenticator doesn't offer that option.

Key points:

- These days cloud-based backup and file-sharing solutions are cheap and plentiful. Use at least one, but consider using all of them if you're serious about running a product creation business.
- Beware of the limitations of WordPress when used in its basic format. It's best used with membership plugins for the purpose of secure digital product delivery.
- Get acquainted with BookFunnel if you like a simple life; it's very reasonably priced and definitely not just for authors.
- Start as you mean to go on in your business, with security measures a core part of your activity.

7

GOING IT ALONE WITH PRODUCT DELIVERY

You'll know already that I'm not a big fan of building your digital product business on a third-party platform. I have qualified that by saying it's fine to list on eBay, Amazon, Teachable and other sites which I'll be mentioning throughout this book, so long as you always preserve that mother ship website, the foundations of your online business which you control and which nobody can take away from you.

In this chapter, I'm going to discuss how you can take payments on the website that you can control. When I take a closer look at some of the third-party platforms that I recommend later in the book, you'll see how they manage payments on your behalf. That can, of course, make your life easier because it removes a tier of hassle from your life online. Beware the seduction of luxury, I know so many people – myself included – who have lost a lot of income from locked or frozen accounts.

Below a selection of popular options for taking payments directly, along with some thoughts and occasional warnings based on my personal experiences. By the way, you always have to pay a fee when you use a payment processor and you should do your due diligence when it comes to that matter, making sure that your pricing allows for the costs of using the service.

VAT MOSS

I am not an accountant, and this is not financial advice. I need to remind you of that before I get started.

When VAT MOSS was introduced in the UK, it was a Chicken Licken moment for all digital marketers. MOSS stands for Mini One Stop Shop by the way, which sounds cute; it isn't.

As a seller of digital products, it meant that I was supposed to charge customers VAT at the rate in which it is applied in their country. Oh, and that's for every EU member state. Fortunately, it doesn't apply elsewhere. Now, I'm just a small, kitchen table business, I don't know about you, I don't have time to mess about with all that.

There is some good news. A 10,000 Euro threshold now applies, so if you don't sell too much stuff, you're fine. I sold that amount this month, so it's not very useful to me.

I stepped back from digital product creation when that rule was originally introduced and, after a short time, digital sales platforms adapted in a way that they managed the VAT element of my digital sales, rather than me. Because I am based in the UK, I only recommend products which manage the VAT MOSS for you, with no hassles whatsoever. I recommend that you do not get embroiled with managing this issue manually, on a transaction-by-transaction basis.

By the way, just like GDPR, you can't bury your head in the sand if you're based in the USA or elsewhere. You need to pay attention to this stuff and make sure your business is compliant if you sell to the EU. Consider yourself warned.

PayPal

This is the online payment processor that everybody's heard of, even your mum. It's well-known, highly trusted and widely available. Virtually everybody in the world has used eBay, which means they're also likely to have used PayPal as the payment processor for their transactions.

The advantage of PayPal is that trust factor; there's wide recognition as a trusted brand, many people have an account, so it's an obvious choice to use, right? Wrong. Sorry to be the bearer of bad news.

PayPal is great, it is simple, and it makes life extremely easy for many online cash transactions. But it comes with many issues for those of us who sell digital products online.

If you do this successfully, at scale, you may well have the rather wonderful experience of seeing hundreds of purchases taking place every day, over a long period of time. It's wonderful when it happens, but if you often use PayPal for the occasional eBay purchase, your account may well get flagged for potentially fraudulent activity and either locked or blocked.

I have been temporarily blocked in the past for just this reason, my only crime being that I made too many sales over too short a period. In that scenario, I lost potential income while my account was in dispute, but I know an online marketer who had it worse. PayPal retained over £10,000 of his earned income, claiming it was fraudulent. I hasten to add that it absolutely wasn't. To mitigate this potential problem, I never retain funds in PayPal, they're removed as soon as they arrive.

The other problem with PayPal is that, as sellers of digital products in the UK, we're liable to pay VAT MOSS on digital products. PayPal has a cumbersome system for dealing with this issue; you have to manually enter the VAT rates for the countries which you may or may not sell in. I don't know about you, but that's an unhelpful solution as far as I'm concerned.

A little further on in this chapter, I will tell you how I cope with this issue. However, for now, this is my line on PayPal. It's great, simple, well-liked and offers simple tools to create payment links and buttons. It's great for paying people and receiving payments from other people, but it has serious limitations for selling digital products at scale.

Finally, I should point out that if you do intend to run a product launch which is likely to be very busy from a sales point of view, it's worth a phone call to PayPal to warn them that they'll be seeing rapid and increased activity on your account and talking them through the reasons for this. I have done this, and it does work, and they're very nice at PayPal, unless they're locking your account without good reason.

One last thing. If a customer disputes a purchase, that can also create issues for you in PayPal. Disputes are usually caused because you found yourself a customer who can't follow the download instructions. If they get shirty and bypass your support system, they can cause problems for you by raising a formal dispute. PayPal will want you to get back to them with a good explanation as to how the situation is resolved. My strategy is to refund, in all situations. Just give them their money back and walk away, it's seldom worth the trouble of a challenge.

Stripe

Stripe is my preferred online payment experience as a user; it's extremely simple to use and it remembers your payment card information, making the purchase process frictionless and fast, which is exactly as it should be.

It's less well set up for straightforward use on your own website, and is best used in conjunction with WooCommerce on a WordPress site (more on this later). However, I use it as my payment processor of choice when I make book sales directly to customers via BookFunnel and it has proven seamless and robust.

If I had a wish for Stripe it would be that they offered more button and widget resources themselves, rather than leaving it to other people to create these integrations.

GoCardless (for more traditional transactions)

I mention this option because there may be a scenario in which you wish to set up direct debit payments; a corporate environment would likely prefer this option to PayPal. This is a bank-to-bank payment option.

I have used it mainly as a customer. I used to pay an accountant using GoCardless and I subscribed to a digital and physical magazine using the service. If you've ever gone through the hassle of setting up an old-school recurring payment with your bank, it's old-fashioned and antiquated. If something in my business requires paper and pen, it gets the heave-ho as soon as possible.

GoCardless is the method we should all be using to set up those recurring standing orders and direct debits. It's simple and seamless and those recurring payments can be cancelled directly by customers without the need for phone calls or human intervention. Finally, GoCardless operates in a number of international territories.

Cryptocurrencies

I like to show that I'm slightly ahead of the curve, so it's important that I mention taking payments by cryptocurrencies on this page. If you're not sure what a cryptocurrency is, without getting too down and dirty, it's a type of virtual or electronic money. Bitcoin is perhaps the best known cryptocurrency at the time of writing, but there are many other crypto options available too.

The best place to go to manage your crypto payments – and by that, I mean converting crypto receipts into cash then transferring to a bank account – is at coinbase.com.

Coinbase even gives you ready-made crypto payment buttons, just like PayPal, and it integrates with WooCommerce, so you can use these buttons on your own website. Plot spoiler: WooCommerce is going to be what I recommend at the end of this chapter.

You may think that taking cryptocurrency payments is a little cutting edge for you at present but remember that people once said the same thing about PayPal and cashless payments. It's coming people, now is the time to get ready.

Payment terminals for in-person sales

I love the 21st Century, it's an incredible time to live and be in business. Occasionally, I get wheeled out to run corporate training events and when I do, they're a great opportunity to sell paperback books directly to customers.

To enable me to do this, I use the PayPal Here card reader, which integrates with an app on my phone and allows me to take secure card payments in person. Now, I'm a child of the seventies and let me tell all you millennials who take this stuff for granted, that is amazing.

The PayPal Here card reader costs less than £50 and is a breeze to use. I see people on market stalls and car boot sales, and they don't have these devices; why not? As far as I am concerned, they have completely revolutionised person-to-person sales.

But hang on a minute Paul, I hear you cry. Selling books in person is not a digital product, so why are you mentioning it on these pages? Well, because we manage this business digitally, my paperbacks are print-on-demand, so I don't need to keep a pile of physical copies in my garage. If I'm running an event, I just order the copies that I'm confident of selling, that way I don't end up with physical stock I can't sell. And here's a ninja tip I learned from one of my podcast listeners. If you're appearing at a conference or event abroad or in another city, so that you can travel light, send the paperbacks to a nearby Amazon locker and pick them up at your location, rather than carrying them with you and making your luggage too cumbersome. What did I say about living in the 21st century? It's brilliant.

By the way, PayPal isn't the only company which sells these devices, so do look around before you buy. However, PayPal does benefit from being such a well-known and trusted brand. Other suppliers include iZettle, SumUp and Square.

Best of the rest

This is by no means an exhaustive list of payment services, but it does reflect the providers I use in my own business. I have tried many more, but the list in this chapter is what I have settled on for the reasons given.

It's worth me mentioning some payment processors which are widely used by other people and which have a good reputation, in the interests of giving you plenty of choices:

- Square – modern, slick, great reputation and impressive innovation. Worth checking out. Already mentioned above as a provider of payment terminals.
- Google Checkout – not really what you want for frequent/mass online sales but trusted and recognised and definitely worth consideration.

Finally, I should say that I have a personal dislike of Sage Pay, Worldpay, Authorize.Net and 2Checkout, either because I've used them as a payment processor and they're more complicated or less featured than they should be, or because I dislike the interface as a customer.

Don't let that put you off taking them out for a spin, but you are reading this book for my take on the issue and that's my personal opinion on the matter.

WooCommerce

You'll notice that I haven't made an unequivocal commitment to any one payment service so far. That's because I've had my fingers burned too many times. I love them all, but I don't trust them. I have found many of these third-party businesses to be like petulant children, locking services and denying access on a whim. In matters of suspected fraudulent activity, I have no problem with that; my issue is with the speed at which these blips are dealt with. A day of lost online sales can be worth hundreds, even thousands of pounds. So, much as I like the payment processors listed above, I won't rely on any single one of them, because that makes my business too vulnerable. Instead, I prefer to use the WooCommerce plugin on a WordPress website, and that enables me to integrate all of these services on one site, allowing the customer to select which they prefer. And, if you fall out with one of those payment processors, you simply replace it with another, selecting from the multitude of WooCommerce integrations, so that your customers will barely notice you made the switch.

This is my preferred business model: sell from a website you own and operate, use a variety of payment options in an integrated way so that you're not reliant on any one of them. That way you build in resilience.

The problem with listing your products on a third-party website is that if you have to move elsewhere, it's as disruptive to your business as moving to a new house. Everything has to change; you have to burn the old house down and start again. If you build your mother ship using WordPress and WooCommerce, you're indestructible. Sure, list products elsewhere if you want to, but always direct new customers back to the mother ship and train them to buy from you directly.

WooCommerce is a free plugin for WordPress websites which allows you to take payments directly from your website, using third-party payment processors. PayPal is baked into the free plugin, but additional services are paid for. You can integrate with pretty well any payment service on the planet, it really is that good.

Key points:

- Payment processors make you vulnerable to account lockouts, so never use just the one.
- My recommended options are PayPal, GoCardless, Stripe and Coinbase.
- Integrate a range of payment processors on your mother ship WordPress website and use the WooCommerce plugin to facilitate their seamless integration.

8

DIGITAL SALES PLATFORMS

So far, I've been incredibly strict about the importance of listing your digital products on your own website. This is what allows you to control your destiny, it means that nobody can take your business down. However, with that security in place, it makes sense to use the third-party platforms at your disposal to find new prospects and customers for your business.

If I sound like I've been a bit down on third-party services, I'm really not, it's just that I'm wise to the vulnerability they can create in your business. And with a defensive plan in place, it's fine to go ahead and use them, making the most of their very considerable benefits.

My policy is then, to always have a mother ship in place where you can sell products directly and lure over your customers. But there's another big issue in setting up a digital products business that we haven't tackled yet – finding customers.

When I teach people about web marketing, I like to start with a simple yet challenging formula for online success:

Traffic x Conversions = Results

That is the secret to business, summed up in three words and two mathematical symbols. Think of traffic as prospects, potential customers, eyeballs on your products. If you don't have that you can't possibly sell anything. It can come in the form of magazine or newspaper readers, radio listeners, TV viewers or in our case, web users.

Next comes conversions and this refers to the number of people who you manage to convert from browsers to buyers. If you send that traffic to a blank web page, you'll get 0% conversions, because they can't buy from you. If your sales page is superb, you'll get 100% conversions, but just to set your expectations at the correct level, that never happens.

When I started working with FC, he told me to take a 1% conversion as a baseline for testing and improving: that's one sale from every 100 viewers of our offer. It doesn't sound very exciting, does it? That conversion rate is closer to reality than anything higher.

So, when we sell digital products, we're always seeking lots of traffic (potential buyers) and an offer that converts browsers to buyers as effectively as possible. Get both right and you make a lot of cash. The problem with listing every-thing on your own website is that it won't have any web traffic when you get started and it's unlikely to convert well either. Getting sales offers to convert prospects to buyers is an art form and if you could get it right every time, there would be a lot more billionaires walking the planet. So, we need a helping hand. That's where digital sales platforms come in; they can certainly help with the traffic element of that simple equation and often, they'll even lend a helping hand with conversions. All we need to do is to find our initial customers on these portals, then move them effectively into buying from us directly.

I'll deal with this process in more detail later in the book, but for now, here is a selection of my preferred digital product platforms along with some of my thoughts as a user.

Amazon

Within the context of this book, I'm only looking at Amazon as a platform for digital sales, but it is quite clearly an excellent place to sell physical products too, via FBA (Fulfilment by Amazon). With that said, I'm looking at selling ebooks, paperback books, hardback books and audiobooks via this marketing platform, and to do that I'm using Kindle Direct Publishing and Amazon's ACX website (Audiobook Creation Exchange).

There are some very big advantages to listing on Amazon:

- Everybody who browses on Amazon goes there to buy – you can't say that about Google (they go to browse) or Facebook (they go to be social).
- Amazon tests, tests and tests again when it comes to optimizing web page conversions – it is a ninja at getting you to buy.
- Amazon has an internal recommendation engine which will suggest your products to customers who are most likely to want to buy them.
- Amazon handles all payments, customer queries and refunds, paying you directly to your bank account as reliable as clockwork.
- Amazon has millions of customers with their

credit cards connected to their accounts, all primed and ready to buy.

- Amazon offers an affiliate programme which enables you to make more money by promoting your products (more on affiliate programmes later).
- VAT MOSS is managed for you.
- Best suited for fiction and non-fiction books in any format, ebook, paperback, hardback or audiobook.

ClickBank

ClickBank is probably the best digital sales platform that you probably never heard of. This is where I listed Auto Cash Funnel, the product that delivered my first six-figure launch. Through FC, I got to mix in the upper echelons of ClickBank digital marketers at the end of the 20th century and as a result, I learned many of their secrets.

ClickBank is not as effective as it used to be for managing massive product launches, but as a digital sales platform, I love it. Here's why:

- ClickBank handles all payments, customer queries and refunds, paying you directly to your bank account.
- ClickBank is used to handling fast and furious sales; you don't get locked down by them in the middle of a big launch.
- ClickBank allows you to remarket to your customers, a follow-up technique which I adore and recommend (more on this later).
- ClickBank has one of the best affiliate schemes,

allowing the product creator complete flexibility in commission levels set.

- ClickBank allows you to reach a global marketplace.
- ClickBank helps you to set up sales funnels if you have multiple digital products to sell.
- You can set up recurring payments for memberships.
- VAT MOSS is managed for you.
- Best suited for training products, software and non-fiction books.

JVZoo

If you can't make a sale on JVZoo, you can't make a sale. I really mean that – it is the digital marketer's paradise. I used the platform to run a couple of six-figure launches, as well as one or two five-figure launches, and JVZoo delivered every time. Here's why I like it so much:

- It has an incredible marketplace of buyers and affiliates.
- It delivers your digital products for you, meaning the customer always gets what they bought.
- It has an amazing affiliate infrastructure, which can help to solve your traffic problem for you.
- It's easy to set up with sales funnel creation made simple.
- You can set up recurring payments for memberships.
- It connects with PayPal and Stripe, two of my recommended payment processors.

- It's built for fast and furious product launches.
- Can automatically calculate and apply sales tax and VAT for all regions, but it is a limited manual operation rather than my preferred automated type.
- Best suited for software and digital training products.
- Includes simple mailing list integration.

Payhip

I use Payhip to sell digital versions of my books directly through BookFunnel and Stripe. I would not use it for a big product launch, it's best for steady sales. It has an easy to use interface, it is ideal for beginners and it creates very nice sales pages and buy buttons without having to get overtechnical. Here are its main selling points:

- VAT MOSS managed for you.
- Simple interface, no technical knowledge required.
- Integrates with BookFunnel.
- You can set up recurring payments for memberships.
- Wonderful payment process.
- Has an affiliate programme.
- Promotes social sharing with a 10% discount option.
- Simple mailing list integration.
- Offer coupons to customers.

Teachable

There are several alternatives available if you want to create an online membership site, but Teachable is by far my preferred option if you decide not to deliver it yourself via a WordPress website.

I have built many membership sites on WordPress and I must admit that Teachable replicates the process so well, that for speed, I will often use Teachable to deliver online training. Here's why I like it so much:

- VAT MOSS managed for you.
- Coupons and discount codes available.
- Excellent support if you've never created an online course before.
- Fabulous sales page creation options.
- Simple money management.
- An online course marketplace.
- Simple, intuitive linking of related courses.
- Mailing list integration.
- Wonderful, clear, sequential training delivery.
- Quizzes and course certificates.

Best of the rest

The list above reflects the services I use – or have used – myself; it is definitely not exhaustive. However, you can manage every scenario I discuss in this book using one – or all – of those options. There are some others worthy of mention, and I'll give brief details on them here, along with my thoughts. Just because I don't use them doesn't mean they're not good, it's more an indication that I just found something that suits me better.

Selz – An excellent alternative to Payhip, which integrates with BookFunnel. Offers simple VAT MOSS management, along with some superb marketing tools and support services. Great for digital products and includes a software licence key option, if you decide to sell software. I would describe it as an integrated online sales platform. If you're creating a shop-type business, Selz is well worth a look.

Shopify – I have no personal experience of Shopify, other than working with several corporate clients who use it. It's used widely, is very popular, but I don't like it because it makes you dependent, and I don't like dependency on any one service for the reasons I've given you already. It gives you everything you need – templates, marketing, checkout and so on. That's great, but what if you built a huge business on it and they changed their terms in a way that was detrimental to your business? So long as you can answer that question with confidence, by all means, use the service, there's certainly nothing at all wrong with it. I include BigCommerce, Ecwid and Magento in this line of thought too. They're all great products, feel free to use them, but always have that mother ship built in the background ... just in case.

E-junkie – Once upon a time this was the go-to site for digital sales and I'd certainly recommend that you check it out. There's nothing wrong with it, it does all the things you'd want it to do – digital delivery, affiliate programmes, coupon codes and so on – it's just that the time was never right for me to use it. It even has a marketplace, so it does come as recommended, even though I haven't used it yet in my own business. It's only the management of VAT MOSS that puts me off this site; like PayPal, they need to manage this better.

Thinkific – An alternative to Teachable which I actually prefer, but they don't handle VAT MOSS as simply as Teachable does. I won't mess around with VAT MOSS; if a system doesn't make it easy for me as a UK resident, it's toast.

Udemy – This is an excellent source of courses to use as a learner, but there's an important lesson to be taken from Udemy's past which should encourage you away from it as a course host – unless you're happy with things as they are, of course. When I started using Udemy years ago, course hosts set their own prices, and many were doing very well on the platform. One day, Udemy announced that it was restricting course prices to within a certain range and all those high-ticket teachers lost the shirt off their back. When you build your business on a third-party platform, you're always vulnerable to rule changes like that. Build a mother ship people, remember what I told you.

Key points:

- Amazon, Payhip and Teachable are my preferred platforms and are most suitable for anybody getting started in the business of creating and selling digital products.
- If you're shifting hundreds or thousands of units, look at ClickBank, Teachable and Amazon. JVZoo is let down by poor VAT MOSS management.

- Two big warnings here – make sure VAT MOSS is integrated into the service that you use and always remember to build your mother ship if you're considering going all-in with a particular service.

9

OUTSOURCING

When I started creating and selling digital products, my mindset was that I had to do everything myself. That created a lag in skills. I couldn't do everything myself, therefore I either had to manage as best as I could with the skills I had (have you ever seen my graphic design work in an art gallery?) or suffer the time delay while I sourced training and learnt how to do the job myself.

As my work progressed with FC, I discovered a wonderful new thing called outsourcing and I've been a big fan ever since. The simple premise with outsourcing is that you don't have the time or the skills to do everything yourself therefore you should pay somebody else to take care of those tasks.

On that first launch with FC, we outsourced the graphics work, the sales copy and promotional email writing, the joint venture partnership sourcing (I'll say more about joint venture deals later) and the product support. You might ask what was left for us to do. Well, I created all the web pages, recorded the sales videos and made the product. FC pretty well outsourced the lot in exchange for his mentorship and experience; without that, there would have been no six-figure launch, so it was a good deal for everybody involved.

It was worth us paying $10,000 for our sales copy because every 1% you can increase conversions is a fistful more of dollars into your pocket. By increasing our initial conversion rate from 1% to 4.5%, we increased our income by more than 300%. So, was the $10k copywriter worth it? Of course, it was, however much it terrified me at the time. Just a note to add, I would only ever have done that under FC's mentorship and guidance. As it turned out, my own copy did pretty well and I wrote the sales pages after that, with FC's input and tweaks.

Since delivering that launch in 2010 outsourcing has become more prevalent and much cheaper and accessible. Do not even consider spending $10k these days, it simply isn't necessary.

You should use outsourcers to do the following tasks:

- Jobs you can't do yourself.
- Jobs you don't want to do.
- Routine, time-consuming tasks which are not a good use of your time.

I outsource work frequently and I've outsourced some unusual things in the past:

- My podcast graphic design was outsourced.
- All promotional graphics for my product launches were outsourced to an excellent graphic design artist in the Philippines.
- The cover for this book, and every other book I have published on Amazon, was outsourced.
- I outsource my book editing and proofreading.

- I once outsourced translation of a book advert from English to Chinese.
- My podcast jingle voice-overs were outsourced.
- I created my Fast Fan Pages software using the services of an excellent outsourced coder who I never met in person.
- I once hired a salesman to make direct calls on my behalf.

As I learnt more about outsourcing, I refined the process so that I now use a collection of services which I deploy for different types of job. There are many more to choose from than I have included in this list, so hunt around online if you want more, but I use these in my own business and can vouch for them:

Fiverr

Weblink: fiverr.com

My notes: This is where you should start as a new outsourcer. I use this website all the time for small jobs which are low-cost, short and simple. Prices start at $5 and I advise you to treat it like eBay; look for well-used services which have lots of positive reviews.
If you're getting graphics work done, always confirm with the vendor that you have copyright clearance to use the image. If in doubt, you buy the image and send it over to the contractor.
I use Fiverr for 3D book cover graphics made from cover images which I supply, for voice-over audio in my podcast, for occasional foreign text translations and for a rather excellent and very cheap book promotion service.

Upwork

Weblink: upwork.com

My notes: Use this website for much more substantial jobs which require a contractor with verifiable and professional experience.

This is the site where I found the excellent coder who built my Fast Fan Pages software service and we worked together for a couple of years.

I securely paid thousands of dollars of invoices through this website and found it invaluable for sourcing great talent and managing the financial dimensions of more demanding projects.

When hiring a freelancer on Upwork, it's a good idea to start with a small job, in order to gauge their skill level and communication. If they prove themselves, then consider hiring them for a bigger project. Beware of big promises and low delivery.

People Per Hour

Weblink: peopleperhour.com

My notes: Like Upwork, this is a good site to use for more substantial jobs, I have used it successfully on many occasions. I tend to go to Upwork first but prioritise People Per Hour if the job requires a native English speaker or a UK-based contractor.

I once paid a freelancer to show me how to set up and operate Google retargeting, recording the session as a tutorial for my future reference. This was money well spent; I have used this valuable skill many times since.

This is also where I found my UK-based salesman, who made calls to bricks and mortar businesses on my behalf for an app project which I haven't even mentioned within these pages yet. To cut a long story short, I won some prize money to develop an app idea. It hit a dead end on technical and funding grounds, but it was fun while it lasted.

Virtual assistants (VAs)

I have never gone quite as far as employing my own virtual assistant, but I have shared several in partnership with others.

A virtual assistant is somebody who you (usually) employ on a freelance basis, full or part-time, who works alongside you in the business, mostly from a base somewhere else in the world.

Here is how I have used virtual assistants in the past:

- When FC and I worked together, FC used a VA to run the helpdesk and we liaised frequently over support questions and queries.
- FC and I also shared the costs of his new VA in the Philippines when we did some of our later product launches and her help was invaluable for me in summarising my how-to videos as PDF guides with screenshots.
- When I managed a project to create a suite of marketing plugins for sale on JVZoo, I worked with a VA to coordinate marketing jobs and plugin testing activities.
- On the same internet launch, we used a team of VAs to supply product support and I worked with

them to provide the product guidance to allow
them to provide detailed support.

I have spent considerable time learning about virtual
assistants and the best places to source them and to speed
things up for you, make a start by checking out 123employ-
ee.com and virtualstafffinder.com. Also, the best book that
you can buy on this topic is *Virtual Freedom* by Chris Ducker,
it's an excellent guide to the world of outsourcing.

Key points:

- Don't do everything yourself; get used to
  outsourcing.
- Always do your due diligence with outsourcers,
  check for testimonials and feedback and be
  prepared to kiss a few frogs along the way.
- If you grow and scale your business, consider
  using a virtual assistant or a team of virtual
  assistants. Do some research first, look before
  you leap.

10

STRATEGIES TO BOOST DIGITAL PRODUCT SALES

Having been involved with many product launches over the years, I'm firmly convinced that the quality of your marketing is more important than the quality of the product itself. However, if the product is rubbish, you'll make great sales once and then customers will give you a wide berth in future, so releasing poor quality products is a short-term strategy from a business point of view.

My personal aspiration is to produce products that are as good as I can make them, and then deploy the best marketing techniques in order to sell them. At this point I want to introduce you to one of the most important questions of digital product creation:

Is it good enough to ship?

I've met so many people who paralyse themselves by seeking perfection; they won't release a product because it's 'not quite right'. I'm all about shipping products. Get it made, get it launched, get it selling, that's my mantra. I believe that when a product hits a certain threshold of quality – it's been checked and proofread – then any amount of polishing will only improve it by a marginal amount. If there is anything wrong with it, you'll soon find that out by getting it launched. And if there is something wrong with it, it's not like we're carving statues out of marble. We can put the error right and replace the file. The only question you have to ask yourself is, is it good enough to ship?

If it is, it's time to get it out there and start the marketing. Believe me, you can have the best product in the world, but if you don't get the marketing right, you'll be the only person who ever knows about it.

Your sales blueprint

What if I could give you the secret to making hundreds and thousands of online sales? Well, the good news is I have already in chapter 8, and it's simple. However, although the formula is straightforward, the mastery of it might take you a lifetime and will constantly change as the world changes around us. Here is a reminder of that magic formula:

Traffic x Conversions = Results

It looks so simple sitting on a page like that, but there are so many ways you can deliver that web traffic and there's so much learning and testing that goes into figuring out how to get sales offers to convert browsers into buyers. I've already dealt at some length in chapter 8 with how you can list your products in third-party websites to find potential buyers for your digital products. Let's take a look now at some of the main things you need to consider when it comes to marketing your products and making them convert well.

Social media

The most obvious source of free web traffic these days is social media. In my internet marketing launches, which weren't that long ago, we didn't use social media at all. It seems incredible to write those words, but it's absolutely true, social media played no part whatsoever in those early six-figure launches. However, that's not true about launches nowadays, social media is at their core.

The first bit of bad news to break to you is that endlessly posting about your products on Twitter, Facebook or LinkedIn is unlikely to pay dividends. All you'll do is annoy your friends. You might get lucky and make the occasional sale, but a sustainable business will not be found in that territory.

Paid social media ads can be extremely effective and I have tried them all: LinkedIn, Twitter, Facebook and Instagram. Here are my thoughts:

- Facebook ads – when you get them working, they're amazing and are my most recommended social media promotion channel. At the time of writing, I am selling thousands of copies of a 0.99 box set of fiction books (in multiple currencies) and I'm generating five-figure sales from that. It's not as easy as it sounds though, you have to make a great offer, target the correct audience on Facebook and make sure your image and promotional text works well. This strategy can also be used effectively with remarketing (see below). Make sure you follow the rules when promoting on Facebook, they can and will block your account

if they have a problem with something you're
doing.

- Twitter ads – plenty of activity from these ads but
  few sales and too expensive to use with low-cost
  products. Poor audience targeting options
  compared to Facebook.
- LinkedIn ads – great business-level targeting but
  expensive to use with low-cost digital products.
  Great for finding consulting clients or if selling
  high-quality, corporate products.
- Instagram ads – don't go there. Unless you're
  selling a highly visual item, I've yet to work with
  anybody who was generating anything more
  than a lot of likes on Instagram. Likes are a vanity
  metric; sales keep the lights on in your business.
  This is not to say that Instagram ads never work,
  they're just not a priority with digital products
  unless you work in a very visual medium i.e. you
  share your fabulous artwork on Instagram and
  then promote your online course teaching
  people how to produce similar artwork.

Google ads

I've dabbled with Google ads many times in my digital
marketing career and I would never claim any level of
expertise with them. As a rule of thumb, I'd recommend
avoiding them unless you're selling high-price items which
allow you a good profit margin and therefore more scope to
'take a hit' while you're fine-tuning the ads to get them to
work. The other scenario in which I would use them is if
you're making so many sales that you are cash-rich in your
business and you can afford to outsource to an agency.

My favourite way to use Google ads is for remarketing which is a much more forgiving way of harnessing this powerful beast. More on remarketing below, but I have always achieved much better results deploying this element of the Google marketing suite and it requires less expertise on my part. It's also considerably cheaper than bidding on keywords for adverts, so a more suitable starting point for the owner of a kitchen table business.

Joint venture (JV) promotions

This is the only strategy we used to create our six-figure launches in internet marketing and if you've never heard of this technique, it's a hidden world of mystery for most people. Joint venture partners are fellow entrepreneurs or businesses in your niche area who will promote your products to their customers, in exchange for a commission or a reciprocal promotion. Clusters of JV partners at the same level tend to get together because promoting each other is of a well-matched and mutual benefit.

One of the many advantages of learning the trade from FC is that he was part of a UK inner circle of big-hitting internet marketers who were dominating ClickBank at that time. These were some of the biggest marketers in the entire internet marketing world, which is why we made thousands of lucrative sales when they promoted our products.

Here's an important lesson about marketing; you always have to pay for it somewhere down the line. To get these massive marketers to promote for us, we gave away 50% or more in commissions, which meant we all generated a lot of income from the product launches. Similarly, when it was time for us to promote their launches, we made those commissions too. The best way to describe a joint venture arrangement is as a 'you scratch my back, I'll scratch yours' scenario. It relies entirely on mutual benefit.

You can set up these arrangements in any industry, but for the purposes of this book, I'll add some links to the key JV sites at Create-Digital-Products.com.

Your promos

Just a note about anything that you use to promote your offers. If the ad images, text or marketing message don't work, it won't send any web traffic to your offer. When people moan about advertising channels being ineffective, it usually means that their ads weren't tested well enough to be certain they were working properly. That often takes a bit of budget wastage, spending money while you're trying to figure out what's working and what's not.

Often marketers give up too soon; the truth is it takes lots of tweaking and testing to get a promotion right. When you do, it becomes a money machine, and that's the kind of ad you're after.

So, when an ad isn't working, review all the elements, test and tweak. Alter the text, the images, the CTA or call to action (i.e. 'Buy now!', 'Find out more ...', 'Grab this offer!' etc), the audience and whatever other parameters you can experiment with. When I worked with FC we used to do this until I was tearing my hair out, but it made a massive difference to the number of sales we made, so was worth every minute of my time that I spent on it.

This process is called A/B split testing by the way. Change one thing at a time – the headline, the image, the CTA – then compare the results with the previous version; was it better or worse? Do more of what gets great results, do less of what creates poor results.

Call to action (CTA)

It's worth a few words about your call to action. Regard the viewers of your web pages like children in a sweet shop. They're looking all over the place: one minute at the sherbet lemons, then at the jelly babies, then at the bonbons. They have a low attention span.

A CTA on a web page tells your prospects what to do next – click here, find out more, claim this offer – the words you use should be:

- Active i.e. DO something
- Specific and concise
- Repeated throughout the page
- Monomaniacal

I always remind clients that if they're not really sure what the purpose of their sales page is, there's no chance their prospects will either. What do you want them to do? Decide on one thing and stick to it. You want them to do whatever leads to the sale – so click here, buy now, add to cart are all great options.

Finally, in the spirit of A/B split testing, experiment with different CTAs on your sales page and see which works best.

Sales pages

Your sales page is the most important part of the sales process, after sending lots of web traffic to your offer via a great advert. The reason for this is that it is responsible for the conversion element of that magic sales formula that I gave you. It's the make or break moment, where we either get them to buy or they walk away.

The importance of a great sales page is why FC was willing to spend $10k on a copywriter who knew all the tricks to get it right. I'm not suggesting for one moment that you spend that amount of money on employing a copywriter, but I have recommended two books at Create-Digital-Products.com which will acquaint you with the key principles of writing great ad copy.

Just like your adverts, sales pages matter – it all matters. You lose prospects at every step in the sales process, the trick is to make your marketing system as frictionless as possible, to convert browsers into buyers.

Always offer generous guarantees with digital products – they don't cost us anything to produce – and take the risk out of the purchase. FC and I offered 30-day money-back guarantees and that de-risked it for the majority of buyers.

We also used an internet marketing ninja trick called an exit splash to try to retain as many of those non-buying browsers and encourage them to buy at a later date. I use a WordPress marketing product called Thrive Themes which is geared to do all the wonderful marketing tricks that you need to succeed in this business. Thrive Themes allows you to set up this exit splash on your WordPress web pages. If you're not using WordPress, use PopUp Domination instead, this product works on regular websites and WordPress.

An exit splash detects when a website user is about to click the X at the top right-hand side of a web page and then pops up an offer before they can leave. It's the online equivalent of asking a customer in a shop if there's anything you can help them with. Exit splashes are flexible and you can also make them appear after a certain amount of time when the website user scrolls down the page and various other options.

At the point where you were about to lose a customer,

this uses an interruption marketing technique to either encourage them to sign up for your email updates or to take a discount code or alternative offer. Getting their details in your email marketing system is best because it gives you more opportunity to convince them to buy your product over a couple of follow-up emails. You have to be relentless with this selling lark, though you've probably figured that out for yourself by now.

Download pages

Your download page is also of crucial importance. This is where your customer accesses the product they just bought from you. Now, you might think it's just a simple page on which you place a couple of links, but I want to urge you to think again.

Your download page should certainly contain those product links, but it's also good practice to congratulate them on their purchase and reinforce that they just made a great decision. If you're up to it, record a short video welcoming them to your training, membership website or whatever it is they just bought.

Always make support links clear, in case of any problems. It's always best they contact you before moaning on social media and damaging your reputation.

Finally, are there any other offers you can add to the download page? Have you written any other books the customer might want to read? Do you have any complementary products they might be interested in? Are you an affiliate for any products which might be a good fit?

When FC and I launched Auto Cash Funnel we made over $10k from a single affiliate offer that we shared on the downloads page. I'd never seen anything like it. If you think about it, you're being made offers like this all the time. When you go to McDonald's, they're always asking you if you want to upsize your portion or add something else to your order. When you're in the line at the pound store, how many times have you been offered a bar of chocolate that you didn't know you wanted? Listen to how many people say 'yes' to that offer, it's all extra profit on a sale that the shop had made anyway. Where can you squeeze a little more profit out on your products' download pages?

Upsells

These offers are known as upsells. They are an easy way of squeezing additional revenue out of a sale you've already made. Think of the stores that offer you batteries for an item you're in the process of buying. It might add up to 20% onto the basic sale; it's well worth having.

Always be alert to potential upsell opportunities, not only on the downloads page but at the point of sale for your main product too. You'll be surprised by how many people buy.

Retargeting/remarketing

This is the marketing strategy that gets me most excited. The first time I ever saw it used it was love at first sight and I've been using it ever since.

Remarketing – or retargeting – is where you visit some-body's web page, then for whatever reason you navigate away from it, and as you move on to other websites, their advertising follows you around everywhere you go. When delegates on my training courses moan to me about how much they hate seeing this, I chide them and tell them to sit up and take notice; this technique works, and they should be deploying it. The first time I used it in testing I generated just short of £2000 in sales on a £499 purchase on a £19 ad spend – how's that for an ROI (return on investment)? This was in a property-related niche where buyers were happy to spend that kind of cash on a product.

I use retargeting on Facebook and Google ads. I have found those channels to be most cost-effective, but you can also deploy the technique with LinkedIn and Twitter. Here is the process:

- Copy and paste the retargeting tag into the <head> area of your website.
- Set up a 'rule' to add everybody who visits your website into a new 'audience'.
- Create ads in Facebook or Google, then deliver them to your newly-created audience.

Everybody who visits your website is pre-sold already i.e. they were on your website for a reason, they must have been interested in something. Retargeting works because it reminds them about your product or service and prompts them to buy. The great thing is – and this is why I like the technique so much – you don't pay unless they click your ad. If they do click your ad, they're familiar with you already so they're more likely to buy. If they don't click your ad, you pay nothing, but you derive benefit from a free, awareness-raising promotion.

There's a reason why so many advertisers use this marketing technique: it works.

Email marketing

Email marketing is the final part of your sales and marketing armoury and it's a topic that you'll need to become familiar with if you're going to enjoy online sales success. This entails prospects and customers giving you their email address so that you can send out marketing emails, newsletters, product launch news, special offers and so on.

Why do you need an email marketing list? Well, everybody on that list is either an interested prospect or an existing customer. This means that whenever you have a new product or service to promote, you have a waiting list of potential buyers nicely lined up in an orderly queue and you don't have to pay any advertising costs to promote to them.

When you get involved in JV partnerships, potential partners will always ask 'how big is your list?' and it becomes an indicator of marketing power and prowess as you progress through your marketing journey.

An email list equates to having customers on demand; build one up as big as you can make it and use it to sell your stuff. At the peak of my internet marketing career, I had a list just short of 25k subscribers. I have around 5k subscribers as an author, but whenever I release a new book, I always make sales. And that is why you must embrace this strategy. Here are the best tools to use to get you started with email marketing:

- MailerLite – offers a free, basic account and is very straightforward to use. Plenty of free training available to get you started – recommended.

- Mailchimp – probably the most widely used service among small business owners but the interface is a bit clunky for my tastes. Offers a free, basic account and plenty of user-friendly training.

Key points:

- Sales and marketing are where your business will flourish or fail. The principles are simple, but never stop learning in this area, there are always new tricks and techniques to be mastered.
- Start building an email marketing list as soon as you can, this will deliver future customers on demand and free you from always having to spend on marketing.
- Become best friends with retargeting, it is an advanced strategy, but boy does it work.

11

MEMBERSHIP SITES & TIERED PRODUCT LAUNCHES

Much of the time, delivery of your digital products will be simple and straightforward. You will be selling a single book, a PDF file, perhaps a how-to video download or something similar. However, I would urge you to think a little bigger than one-time products.

As I progressed through my own online journey, I discovered what's regarded as the holy grail of web-based income: recurring income. The problem with a one-off sale is that it's just that; you make your sale, then you're done. You either have to sell more of that product to more people or make another product.

I soon learned in internet marketing that the industry tended to function in quarterly cycles and that most marketers were having to come up with a new product every three months to sustain their income. That felt like a lot of hard work to me – especially when you were so vulnerable to having a bad launch and therefore reducing your income for a substantial part of the year. It also felt to me that it was a bit 'hamster in the wheel'; the income was great, so long as you kept spinning.

It was at that stage that I pivoted my model to writing, which is the ideal 'do the work once, profit for 70 years after your death' model. I also learned the value of membership websites, offering recurring monthly income.

Now, in the interests of complete transparency, let me explain why I am an enthusiastic cheerleader for membership sites, how I've set up and run a few, but why I don't use it as a model in my own business.

Just like you probably sigh at the thought of writing 23 fiction books, which is my tally at the time of writing this book, so I sigh at the prospect of the constant and ongoing support commitment that would be required in running a membership site. I know, I've dabbled with it in the past. I'm great at building them, I love creating the content for them, but I don't like the support element of this business model. So, I prefer to share my knowledge in the form of books like this; I get to share my tips and experiences, I get to build a website around it, but I don't have to touch a helpdesk.

The best source of information on how to build a membership site is The Membership Guys Podcast which I listen to every week and which makes me want to start a membership site, in spite of hating the support element. Seriously, it's a superb resource, do check it out if this is where your interest lies.

So, with my confession now out in public, why would you consider a membership site?

- Monthly, recurring income from a committed customer base and community.
- Predictability of income over the year.
- 'Tied in' audience who will buy other related products which you produce.

- Building an asset which you could sell or base an exit strategy around.
- A tiered entry website can also be used for product delivery, where a pick 'n' mix purchase option is available (i.e. the customer can buy products 1/2/3, 1 & 2, 2 & 3 or 1 & 3).
- You have a training product which needs to be delivered sequentially over a series of videos, rather than in a single session.

When it comes to creating a membership website, you have two key options: either you can use a third-party service, or you can create your own membership website. I'm only going to discuss the use of WordPress if you select option 2 as, quite frankly, I believe you're barking up the wrong tree if you use anything else.

If you prefer option 1, I'll give you my favourite solution, plus one alternative which has a big Achilles heel if you want to sell in the EU.

Should you want to build up an asset with a view to selling it at some point in the future, use WordPress, so you own and control the membership site.

If you just need a membership site for delivery, for what will be a shorter-term period, use a third-party option.

Teachable

Teachable is by far my preferred third-party option for delivering multi-part training programmes which aren't going to be around forever. It's so easy to use, with such excellent support, it negates the need to create your own platform. Teachable offers the following benefits:

- Simple VAT MOSS management.
- Customisable and flexible sales pages which you can tweak to improve conversions.
- Built-in quizzes, certificates and course compliance checks.
- Feedback options.
- Zapier integration which allows you to securely connect to other services i.e. a helpdesk.
- Marketing and email integrations as well as Facebook pixels.
- Coupon codes for effective promotions.
- Drip content – which means that you can manage content delivery over a period of weeks or months.
- Affiliate promotion options.

Put simply, Teachable allows you to do everything I have recommended in this book, every single ninja marketing trick. When I tried it out for the first time, I immediately loved it, there's nothing quite like it available elsewhere. I know, because I checked out all the main competitors before I committed to Teachable.

The only reason you wouldn't opt for Teachable is if you're building a long-term business, which you intend to sell on as an asset at a future date. Please remember all the warnings I gave you about building your internet kingdom on third-party websites, and how that can potentially make you vulnerable. I have a couple of short-term courses on the platform, I'm completely comfortable with that, but if I was building a long-term business around a membership website, I would not use Teachable for that.

Thinkific

I'll give Thinkific an honourable mention because it would have been my preferred choice if it had done a better job of handling VAT MOSS. It's a little more technical than Teachable, which is why it appealed to me, and it has many more options built into it.

Thinkific is more business class and is suitable for experienced and established marketers. It offers the ability to record your voice-over presentations directly within the software, which instantly removes the cost of Camtasia or any other screen recording software.

It also offers marketing essentials such as countdown timers (great for adding scarcity to your offers), more flexible credit card billing (i.e. seven days/one month free then billed after trial period) as well as upsell options.

In short, Thinkific is fabulous for more advanced users but it fails on an essential item for EU marketers: VAT MOSS management.

Using WordPress as a membership site

At the risk of offending lovers of Drupal, concrete5 and Joomla, I'm not even going to advise that you shop around if you're building your own membership website. Please, save yourself the strife, just build your membership website on WordPress.

I have used WordPress for membership websites and complex product delivery on many occasions now and it steps up to the mark every time. Whatever I want to do, however unreasonable my requirements, WordPress can cope with anything I throw at it. Here's a reminder of the WordPress basics:

- Use SiteGround's WordPress hosting.
- Install your WordPress site in 2 minutes by heading for the cPanel area, then using the Softaculous autoinstaller.
- Install a couple of essential plugins to get things underway – the core (free) plugins I use are Classic Editor, Anti-Spam, All In One WP Security, GDPR Cookie Consent, Head, Footer and Post Injections, SG Optimizer, UpdraftPlus and All In One SEO Pack.

Having set up the WordPress basics, it's time to move on to the look and feel of your website.

Thrive Themes

Just as I stuck my neck out with WordPress, I'm going to stick my neck out with what you should use to determine the style of your membership website. I use the Thrive Themes suite of tools and they are, as far as I'm concerned, the most comprehensive set of advanced marketing tools you could use on your WordPress site. I love Thrive Themes and I use it on most of my websites.

Here's what's on offer from Thrive:

- The best set of marketing tools you'll find anywhere with countdown clocks, exit splashes, simple pixel code insertion, intelligent email marketing, A/B split testing, headline testing, testimonial generators and more. If I mentioned it in this book, you'll find it in Thrive Themes.
- Thrive Architect, a drag-and-drop page builder for WordPress which allows you to get every

single page exactly as you want it to look without being constrained by somebody else's template.
- Built-in membership site creation tool which makes your course creation simple, intuitive and straightforward.

You can either subscribe to Thrive Themes on an ongoing basis or buy the separate plugins as you need them, which is what I tend to do.

OptimizePress

I have used OptimizePress for many years and it pretty well does what Thrive Themes does without some of the nifty extras built-in.

Just like Thrive Themes, OptimizePress is a site builder, which means you can create a website just the way you want it with drag-and-drop page options to help you avoid all coding jobs.

OptimizePress gives you ready-made marketing page templates, so everything is baked in for you. It integrates with all the main third-party services that you'll need and focuses entirely on effective marketing outcomes.

At the time of writing I use both OptimizePress and Thrive Themes. I like to have both up my sleeve so I can use the most suitable option for any given project. I would class both as essential marketing tools, but if you're on a restricted budget and you have to make a choice, opt for Thrive Themes simply to access the cool stuff that they offer.

Elementor

I'll mention Elementor here simply because you've probably heard of it and you may be wondering why I don't recommend it as a site builder for WordPress use.

Elementor is excellent, in that it releases you from the tyranny of coded WordPress site layouts and allows you to do whatever you want on your website. However, although it is superb for general use – it's my recommendation when I teach small businesses how to use WordPress from scratch – it isn't specifically geared to marketing outcomes like OptimizePress and Thrive Themes are.

By all means, check it out for regular website building, but use a bespoke marketing product if it's sales, conversions and internet ninja outcomes that you seek.

Membership site plugins

Whatever you use to determine the look and feel of your WordPress-based membership site, you are going to need to buy another plugin to run alongside OptimizePress or Thrive Themes to deliver and manage the specific membership management elements.

These are the key jobs that membership plugins deal with:

- Creating and managing membership tiers (i.e. beginners, novices, pros or Bronze, Silver, Gold access levels).
- Managing payments via a variety of payment processors (i.e. PayPal, Stripe, ClickBank and JV Zoo).
- Affiliate and coupon code management.

- Set up and manage subscriptions, one-time payments, instalments.
- Quizzes, course certificates and surveys.
- Access level locking, dependent on what the customer has purchased.
- File security – to avoid Black Hat websites accessing your content via an insecure 'back door'.

I have tried a wide variety of membership plugins over the years, there are many of them available and this is not an exhaustive list. However, here are four that I have put through their paces. Always take the free trials where available in order to see which suits you best prior to purchase:

MemberPress – this plugin has a testimonial from The Membership Guys, so if they like it, it must be good. It was certainly on my list of contenders when I was building my own membership website and, looking at the features again now, I suspect it was because it didn't offer ClickBank integration that I didn't use it. For reasons already explained elsewhere in the book, ClickBank is a favourite of mine for payment processing.

WishList Member – very well-known, highly regarded and widely used. I'm quite geeky, but I always found it rather complicated to use and not very graceful in its delivery. I've considered it on several occasions but always found the other options in this section more straightforward to use. As so many people use WishList Member I always felt that I was missing out on something, so please do try it out, just in case I am.

Courseware – this is the plugin I use in my own membership sites. It does everything I want it to, without making any fuss. I'd go as far as saying that it's a good choice for a beginner membership site builder; it doesn't overcomplicate life. I opted for this plugin because I'd seen somebody else's membership website, I liked it, so backwards engineered it so that mine looked the same. It also lets me sell via ClickBank's payment system.

MemberMouse – another popular and widely used membership plugin, simple to use, feature-packed, straightforward to deploy and highly recommended. The only thing that puts me off is the monthly payment plan, I prefer to pay annually for Courseware plugin updates rather than on an ongoing basis. That's a personal preference though.

As a final point, I recommend never using a free membership plugin. You need to select a plugin option that is widely used and properly supported; it's the engine of your membership website and you don't want to experience technical problems. Also, remember The Membership Guys Podcast, this is the best place to go to learn about the topic in depth; I like it so much, I listen to it for fun and personal development.

Key points:

- Teachable is the best way to deliver courses and membership sites if you're a complete beginner.
- If you want to build up a membership site with a view to selling it on at a later date as an ongoing business, use WordPress with Thrive Themes.

- Whichever theme you use on your WordPress site, you will need to use it alongside a membership plugin. Always pay for this; make the most of free trials to test out which plugin best suits your needs.

12

AFFILIATE MARKETING

Affiliate marketing is a thing of great beauty and as a digital product creator you can use the technique in a variety of ways. In fact, if you feel at the end of this book that creating products just isn't for you, no problem, take all of the marketing principles I've shared here and use them instead to sell other people's products as an affiliate. So, before we get overexcited, what is affiliate marketing?

Affiliate marketing is where products or services are promoted and sold by a third party in return for a referral fee, at no extra cost to the customer. That's a triple win situation. The vendor achieves more sales by harnessing an army of affiliates who help to promote their product. The affiliate makes money from a product that they didn't create. The customer receives the same product at the same price, and occasionally at a lower price, as a result of the affiliate arrangement. It also allows the customer to support the person whose blog, podcast or content they consume at no extra cost to them.

Affiliate marketing basics

Becoming an affiliate entails signing up to an affiliate programme. Frustratingly, not every great product has an affiliate programme. Amazon has one – it's called Amazon Associates – and I suggest you join it even if the commissions are quite low.

ClickBank has a great affiliate programme and the product promoters there know how to run a decent promo campaign, offering bonuses and rewards for the most successful affiliates. Commissions are often set at 50% or higher.

JVZoo also has an excellent affiliate scheme for digital products and, once again, marketers on JVZoo know how to create a product which finds buyers. They too offer high commissions.

When you sign up to an affiliate programme, you are given a referral link, which is unique to you. This is how your referral sales are tracked. A regular weblink might look like this: **https://mygreatproduct.com**. An affiliate link will look something like this, with a unique element added that is specific to you: **https://mygreatproduct.com/aff=yourname**.

Affiliate weblinks come in a variety of different formats, but they'll always contain a unique identifier. When you share your unique link, and somebody clicks that link and goes on to buy, the sale is recorded in your affiliate account and you receive a cut on the sale.

Affiliate payouts are always subject to a retention period, which is usually a little longer than the refund window; there would be no point in me paying you your commission immediately if I ended up with five of your customers refunding afterwards, I'd be running at a loss. This also protects against affiliate link cheating, where dishonest affiliates buy from their own link then take advantage of a generous refund guarantee.

Affiliate payouts usually have thresholds too, so you may have to wait until you've accrued £25 or £50 and sometimes more until you can get paid.

Finally, the best affiliate programmes provide banners, graphics, pre-written blog articles and social media posts to help you promote. Internet marketers on ClickBank and JVZoo do this stuff really well; the rest of the world is not so good at it.

How affiliate marketing helps product sellers

Remember that magic formula for making more digital sales? Well, affiliate marketing helps with the traffic element of that. If you team up with the right affiliates with enough marketing power, it can make a huge difference to your income. On all the launches I worked on with FC, we always worked with FC's high-powered affiliate marketing pals. It was them, not us, that took us into the six-figure launches, we could not have done it on our own. We were offering 50% affiliate commissions too, giving away half of the sale price.

At this point, you might protest and shout that there's no way you're giving away 50% of the sale price to other people when you did all the work. Well, good luck with that strategy, you'd better have a huge email list of your own all lined up and ready to go. The simple truth is you generally have to pay for increased web traffic anyway. You're either paying Facebook, or Google, or Amazon or an affiliate. If you manage to team up with the right affiliates, not only will they deliver better results than paid ads, you'll also be able to set things up so that you skim off the emails of your new customers too. Google, Amazon and Facebook won't let you do that (unless you use lead ads on Facebook).

It's not all good news though. Affiliates will soon lose interest in your offer if it doesn't deliver the second part of my magic, moneymaking formula: conversion. If they send lots of their customers to your offer, and they don't make any commissions, they'll quickly ditch you and find something else that does convert.

I test offers all the time on my websites; if they don't make any money, regardless of how much I like the product, they get ditched.

How affiliate marketing saves a lot of work

If you've got this far in the book and you love the concepts that I've shared here, but you can't face doing all the work, fear not! Being an affiliate marketer is actually a job. You can sell products which other people have created and just take your 50% on each sale.

You've probably found blog posts online where somebody has written a list of the 'Top 10' something or other. Well, they're not doing that out of the goodness of their hearts, those are all affiliate products which give them a kickback. They provide value, by creating a great blog post discussing the pros and cons of whatever it is they're reviewing. Then, like wasps to jam, readers who are researching that new product find the blog post online, read it, think to themselves *I like the sound of this one*, click the link and – hey presto – somebody just made a sale as an affiliate.

If you do become an affiliate marketer, and I strongly suggest that you do, then always make sure that you're promoting products that you can personally vouch for.

Never endorse rubbish, it'll ruin your reputation and you'll end up selling nothing. Become a trusted source of recommendations, that's the best way to succeed at affiliate marketing.

Additional affiliate profits

I run a hybrid version of all affiliate marketing techniques. I join every single affiliate programme that I can for the products I use and love, then recommend them across my blog, my podcast and any other outlets I have.

Whenever I create new digital products, I always have an affiliate programme baked into it, with a wide array of promotional materials on offer to help my own affiliates make the most of things.

I generally run my own affiliate programmes through ClickBank, because their system is so trusted, robust and reliable, but I have used JVZoo in the past and I use Payhip's affiliate scheme for my non-fiction books.

Affiliate income is invisible money, it comes in automatically and you don't have to do any of the work. Source some good-fit products and place them wherever you can – without overwhelming us – to generate additional income. I even use affiliate links in PDF guides, because it's so easy to add a banner and embed an affiliate link when creating content in that way.

My affiliate tips & tricks

As with all things in life, there are always tricks to be learned when working as an affiliate. I'll share some of my favourite tips here.

Firstly, the problem with affiliate links is that they're a bit long and ugly in their raw format:

https://mygreatproduct.com/aff=yourname

It's also obvious that it is an affiliate link. Now, we're not trying to deceive anybody here, you should always include a statement prominently that reads something like this:

This post includes affiliate links for which I may make a small commission at no extra cost to you should you make a purchase.

However, we want our shared links to look aesthetically pleasing, also it's quite nice to know which of the promotional channels that you're using is working best. Enter **Pretty Links** a rather fabulous and free WordPress plugin which allows you to create, not unsurprisingly, pretty links.

So, with Pretty Links, an ugly link like **https://mygreatproduct.com/aff=yourname** would easily become:

https://mygreatproduct.com/TW
https://mygreatproduct.com/EM
https://mygreatproduct.com/FB

In this example, we'd use a different Pretty Link to indicate a promotion shared on Twitter [TW], Facebook [FB] and via email [EM]. Pretty Links creates what's known as a redirect link, which does exactly what it says on the tin: it redirects users from your Pretty Link to your affiliate link, without losing you a commission along the way.

We can take this concept one step further with a service called Geniuslink at geniuslink.com. When you promote products on Amazon, there's an immediate problem; depending on where you are in the world, you're supposed to buy through the Amazon store for your country. This is a big problem for me when promoting my books to an international audience. I might share my local amazon.co.uk weblink, but somebody in the US will be asked to buy the product via their dedicated website at amazon.com. That creates friction in the sales process and at that point, many potential buyers will give it up as a bad job.

Geniuslink allows you to create geo-targeted weblinks for Amazon, which cleverly detect where you are in the world, then direct you automatically to the correct buying page. In addition, just like Pretty Links, it allows you to create more attractive and customised promotional links and you can also make multiple versions of those links so that you can see which web traffic source is performing best for you. It's all very clever stuff.

I would advise against the skinflint option of using Bitly or another similar, free service. These often get flagged as spam and I've even known the links to be blocked on Facebook.

My final tip for you is to check out the Affilorama blog and website and start learning more about affiliate marketing techniques and best practice.

Key points:

- However, you decide to approach digital product creation in your own business, make sure you become familiar with the basics of affiliate marketing in order to generate additional, passive income.
- Only promote products which you can personally vouch for; you can easily find a better

product to promote, reputations aren't so easily replaced.

- Make use of affiliate links wherever you can – think laterally – but never overwhelm your customers with adverts. The best affiliate marketing combines excellent products and great content.

13

PRODUCT SUPPORT OPTIONS

I'll be honest with you, the thing I hate most about creating and selling digital products is providing support services. It just doesn't suit my temperament, but then that's why somebody like me needs to use a virtual assistant to manage this stuff.

So, having confessed to you my Achilles heel in this business model, let's discuss why providing support is so important – even if you do hate it.

Product support services are all about reputation management and great customer service. If you have a problem with a payment, delivery of a product or a query about the product itself, you want a fast response if you're the customer. I don't mean that somebody gets back to you within a week or a month. I'm talking about a fast and full response within a reasonable time frame, and that's 24 hours as far as I'm concerned. I say 24 hours because we're all in different time zones, so you have to take account of your need to sleep from time to time.

Much as I hate providing support personally, I want to be clear, I have always provided fast and excellent support for all of my products. As far as I'm concerned, great support is determined by the following factors:

- A speedy response to the initial query.
- Relentless follow-up until the customer is happy.
- Sending a personalised how-to video guide, if it's needed.
- Offering full and fast refunds.
- Never, ever quibbling about refunds.
- Overdelivering to make sure customers are completely happy with their purchase.

There are many ways that you can provide this support, but you should always make provision for it, whatever level you're at in your business. By the way, one of the reasons I love the BookFunnel service is that they provide support. That service is worth every penny I pay for their service as far as I'm concerned.

ClickBank and Amazon deal with first-tier customer support too, though ClickBank will have to refer technical queries to you, focussing instead on the refunds and payment issues.

Here are the best ways to provide product support:

Support emails

The simplest solution is an email address which will be something like support@mywebsite.com. If you use this system, just make sure you will see the emails when they arrive, don't send them to a folder which you never bother to check.

I'm less keen on this option because it gives customers a

direct link to your email inbox; I'd advise a level of separation.

Help desk options

My preferred support option is to offer a help desk and my favourite option is to use Freshdesk which has a more than adequate free option.

Freshdesk gives you everything you need for a basic level of support, such as a ticketing system, tracked replies, a nice widget to add to your website and the ability to create FAQ articles, a fabulous system which helps prevent customers raising queries in the first place.

Many people get excited about Zendesk which I always found to be overcomplicated as a small business user.

Before using Freshdesk, I used the free, open-source software called osTicket which was excellent. You'll find it bundled alongside WordPress with SiteGround web hosting. Hint: just use SiteGround, you won't regret it.

FC used to use a service called Kayako which always seemed to work very well too, and I used this service a lot while we were working together.

There are many other support desk services available, but that little list should steer you in the right direction.

Managed support

When I was working on the WordPress plugin project which was sold via JVZoo, for the first time in my experience, we used an outsourced support service. I liked this set-up, it worked well, but it came with some expense and you need to be generating sufficient sales to justify it.

You'll have to shop around a bit, and there's no particular service that I can recommend at the present time, but you should at least be aware that this is a thing.

Virtual assistants

I've already dealt with using virtual assistants elsewhere in the book, but in this scenario, we're deploying a more specialist VA to manage a particular part of our business. I have used this process on several occasions and where you have a great VA in place, it works like a dream.

Best of the rest

Don't forget that you can use Skype, Facebook Messenger, WhatsApp and any other free service you care to think of when providing customer support. Just be sure that the support requests don't get missed and also that they don't encroach on your personal space, you'll quickly regret it if this happens.

I also recommend downloading the free Jing software from TechSmith, which allows you to take screenshots and record and share very short videos. A picture saves a thousand words when it comes to customer support and, believe me, it's often faster and quicker to record a quick Jing guide rather than getting involved in a long email exchange.

FAQ areas

In most businesses, there are a series of questions which customers will ask you time and time again. These are the FAQs – frequently asked questions – of your business. In order to reduce the number of support requests, compile a handy list of FAQs which customers should consult prior to contacting you. Most of the time, they'll find the answer there.

Our aim is always to reduce the number of support requests we receive; the best approach is to anticipate as much as you can and head it off at the pass.

Refunds

Deploy a no-quibble refund policy. If they're not happy, refund, no questions asked. We don't have postage or delivery costs, we don't hold stock; if a customer isn't happy, proactively refund them. It's not worth the hassle arguing the toss, it'll take up your time and energy.

I want customers to be evangelists for what I do, I don't want them to have a bad experience and I don't want them moaning on social media about poor customer service or terrible response times. This is a privilege of not holding stock; give customers their money back if they want it and let them keep the product too if it makes life sweeter.

There's a more strategic reason for this too; you don't want complaints to PayPal, who will lock up your account if there's an unresolved dispute. You also don't want customers starting chargebacks on credit cards, this will seriously damage your vendor reputation and therefore your business. Just refund, it takes a moment and it makes problems disappear in a cloud of smoke.

Key points:

- Always provide at least one support option, even if it is just via email or Facebook Messenger.
- I recommend an online service such as

Freshdesk. This provides a degree of separation between you and the customers, but most importantly creates an organised, professional and searchable archive of queries.

- If you really hate providing your own support, buy in a virtual assistant to take the strain or work as an affiliate selling products which you don't have to support.

14

PRESENTATION TOOLS

There are a number of presentation tools which every digital product creator needs to be aware of. Hopefully, you recall me speaking earlier about my six-figure webinar held while I was sleeping during a holiday in Spain, and a joint venture partner was generating that income for us. When you run live webinars, you can then use the recordings to create new products to sell in different ways. That's what we did with 7-Figure Success Formula; it was recorded live, we repackaged and resold it several times.

Here's another interesting thing about live events. Always send out the replay video afterwards. On that six-figure webinar, we made about 45% of the sales from the live event and the remainder from sending out the replay. That's because not everybody can make it to the live event, so you're missing a trick if you don't send it out afterwards, you're leaving money on the table.

I've listed the tools I use – or which are commonly used – below, with my thoughts about them.

GoToWebinar

This is the corporate world's favourite tool for hosting live webinars and it's what FC and I were using for that six-figure webinar. Put simply, it's the best there is. It's also very expensive.

GoToWebinar is robust, reliable and has every basic marketing tool that you need built-in. You can run screen share webinars or front-of-webcam presentations, with Q&A, polls, PDF handouts delivery and paid webinar options all available. It offers personal branding options, customised follow-up emails and Zapier integrations, which allows you to link GoToWebinar with other third-party services such as your email provider.

Years ago, when I first started using it, their video file processing was horrendous, but that was all sorted out long ago and GoToWebinar will now record your presentation and make it automatically available via follow-up email to attendees and non-attendees.

I have tried many webinar solutions and I've never used one that was better than GoToWebinar; it's just the price that may make it prohibitive to you.

Zoom

Zoom is a great alternative to GoToWebinar, mainly on the basis of price rather than service. It does everything that GoToWebinar does at a lower price but in my personal opinion, not quite so well or simply.

The truth is that most people will end up using Zoom due to the more attractive price point and there's absolutely nothing wrong with it. It has had a bit of a chequered past over basic security, but the Zoom team appear to be on top of that now.

If money was no object, I'd use GoToWebinar every time, but Zoom is an excellent alternative and a lot kinder to your pocket.

Facebook Live

Facebook Live is a great way to find a new audience, and that's why I'd recommend featuring it in your marketing mix. The core problem with a webinar is that you can only gather an audience from existing contacts, unless you pay for advertising, which is fine, by the way. However, Facebook Live videos gather an amazing number of views after the main event has passed, so they're an excellent, no-cost way of finding a new audience without having to pay for the privilege.

Facebook Live can be used perfectly well on its own, but it's best used alongside a third-party service like BeLive.TV which allows branding and background options and makes the experience more geared to marketing purposes. BeLive.TV has a free option which will be suitable for most beginner digital product creators.

It's worth mentioning too that if you use Zoom's webinar service, this also links up directly with Facebook Live. That's a nice option because it keeps all your promotion work in one place.

YouTube Live

There's absolutely nothing wrong with going live on YouTube, but I don't use it personally for two very big reasons. Firstly, you can only really send an existing audience to a YouTube channel, so you're immediately limiting your viewing numbers. Secondly, YouTube is not social in nature in the way that Facebook is, so Facebook always wins as far as I'm concerned.

I tried Google Hangouts in the early days, hated the lag and delay, and moved on quickly. Google will have to do something pretty impressive to bring me back.

WebinarJam & EverWebinar

I purchased this service a couple of years ago because it immediately caught my interest as a superb marketing tool. In the days when I purchased, it was called Evergreen Webinar and I loved it from the get-go. That product allowed me to create pre-recorded, as-live webinar presentations using Camtasia, then to market them on demand with every single ninja marketing trick built-in as standard. At one time, I had several of these automated webinars running and people could register for the webinar at any time and it would play out and send reminders as if the event was live. It was a superb marketing tool.

The Evergreen Webinar system evolved to become WebinarJam (for live events) and EverWebinar (for automated, as-live events and replays) and as an early adopter, I was grandfathered in at a low price.

In the early days WebinarJam integrated with Google Hangouts – hence my dislike of them – but they were constantly problematic. All those initial teething problems have now been resolved and both services are the most feature-packed, mega-marketing packages you're likely to find anywhere. However, it's quite pricey but less costly than GoToWebinar. You also have to pay for WebinarJam and EverWebinar individually, which bumps that price up. If you're a serious marketer with resilience in your budget, you won't even blink before you buy. If your budget is restricted, you'll need a cheaper alternative.

WebinarIgnition

The cheaper option is WebinarIgnition, a clever WordPress-based system which you install on your website (I did warn you that you need to use WordPress if you're going to do this properly) at a much lower cost than anything else I've recommended.

WebinarIgnition uses YouTube Live in a clever way which overcomes all my objections about it being a largely neutral marketing platform by integrating it with the kind of superb marketing system deployed by WebinarJam and EverWebinar.

I have used WebinarIgnition – I usually buy these products just to test them and keep my product knowledge up to date – and I love it. It's come on in leaps and bounds since I purchased an early iteration of the plugin and it really is a very impressive budget option.

Key points:

- You're spoilt for choice when it comes to webinar options and there really is something available at every price point.
- Zoom and GoToWebinar are best used for basic live events with follow-up replays; their integrated marketing tools are fairly basic.
- If you can afford it, and you're really serious about this business, look very hard at

WebinarJam and EverWebinar, they offer a suite of marketing tools like no other.

- If you're on a budget, don't feel at all bad about using WebinarIgnition on your WordPress website, it really is very impressive for the price of it.

15

DIGITAL PRODUCT CREATION NEXT STEPS

We're almost there, I'm about to remove the stabilisers from the back wheel and send you out on your own to explore the wonderful world of digital product creation. But before you go, I have some last thoughts to share, information that will further set you up to make a great income from this line of work.

Sales funnels aka product escalators

Why make one sale when you can make many? Don't limit yourself, always be asking how you can get a prospect to buy their first product and when they've made that initial purchase, how you'll get them to make a second, a third, a fourth and so on.

You may feel this doesn't apply to you in your line of digital product creation, whatever topic that happens to be. Let me tell you now that whatever it is you do, there is always more money in the deal.

I'd like you to think of your digital sales business as a

sales funnel or product escalator going forward, whichever image works best for you.

The sales funnel structure involves throwing in lots of prospects into the wide top of the funnel, then moving them progressively towards the narrow end. At the top we have browsers and tyre kickers, people who maybe don't even know us yet and who have not purchased from us. As they move along the funnel – perhaps getting a freebie from you first of all, then joining your email list, then being exposed to a cheap, paid-for related product – we move them towards that focused point down below where the very best, highest-spending customers dwell. These are the fans, the people who don't care what you're charging, they love your stuff and they want your knowledge.

The product escalator concept works the same way, except in this visual analogy, the prospect has to take that first step forward (i.e. download a freebie or purchase a cheap product) to begin moving up the escalator, via products of an ever-increasing price, until they reach the top, where the high-commitment/high-price options dwell, offering things like 1-1 mentorship and mastermind groups.

Here is an example of a basic but well-tested sales funnel/product escalator model:

- Offer a free gift – a PDF file with 10 tips relating to your topic or niche is a great starter. Always offer in exchange for an email address so that you can deliver further/ongoing marketing.
- Offer a cheap, paid-for item which builds on that first gift. The second offer should give away the secrets that the first item teased. At this point, we just want our prospects to spend money with us, even at a low price point.

- It's now time to increase price and commitment – that second product should come with an upsell of some type, perhaps a five-part, paid-for video series.
- The video series will give a discount voucher or exclusive access to your online training programme, delivered via WordPress or Teachable. This could also be access to your membership site.
- Once you have built up a suitable size audience, offer a paid-for online event, followed by a paid-for physical/in-person event, once you're certain you can fill it.
- Now it's time to offer premium price products: 1-1 consultancy, individual or group mentorship or a mastermind group.

Notice how the price goes up every time, but we don't ask our prospect to marry us after a first date. Always try to build in a full or partial funnel when you conceive new digital products. You don't necessarily have to deliver on that full sequence, but always ask yourself, how can you squeeze more income out of a single sale.

I have applied this principle in my fiction writing which you might think has little to do with this style of digital marketing. I write in trilogies with compelling endings so that I can give book one away for free or at a discounted price. I increase the price between book 2 and book 3 and I also make a box set option available which allows me to make a sale on two books at once, rather than two in isolation. I also cross-promote my other trilogies to encourage readers to repeat the experience, only this time, book 1 in the series is not free. The more books I can move them through, the more profit I make on that initial freebie or discounted book.

Recurring income

Please pull out all the stops to create a recurring income. I have made countless mistakes in the process of creating and selling digital products and the biggest was not attending to the matter of recurring monthly income sooner than I did.

Recurring income takes the pressure off you, it means you're not lurching from product launch to product launch, always wondering where next month's income is coming from. Seriously, this is the magic bullet as far as digital product creation is concerned. I strongly recommend aspiring to a monthly-paid membership site if you can sustain that; everything I've ever learned about this business makes that the best, long-term option. A well-run, busy membership site can replace your job and your income and give you a valuable asset to sell when it's time for you to move on.

Evergreen content

With that said, make sure that your content is evergreen in nature, whether it forms part of a membership or some other standalone product. This is another of the harshest lessons you will learn; it's a thankless task having to constantly refresh fast-dating content. I know, I fell into that trap.

In everything you do, ask yourself how you can allow for information changing or going out of date. I have done just that with this book. Instead of listing resources which may not be available by the time you read this book, I am directing you to a web page at Create-a-Product.com which I can update in a matter of minutes rather than having to re-edit and republish a book every few months. How can you make your digital products last longer, without the constant need to update or refresh them?

Recommended resources for further learning

There are four books which I can recommend for further related reading, all of them are on my own bookshelf. The authors know what they're talking about and can prove it with their results:

- *Launch* by Jeff Walker. This is the definitive guide to launching and selling products effectively. As you'd expect, Jeff also has a course available.
- *Platform* by Michael Hyatt. If you have something to sell, this is the book for you. Michael Hyatt gives a comprehensive guide to getting noticed in a noisy world.
- *Virtual Freedom* by Chris Ducker. Already mentioned once, but this book is excellent and a must-read if you're serious about building and scaling your business.
- *The Adweek Copywriting Handbook* by Joseph Sugarman. This book is widely regarded as the copywriting bible; use it to become a master of writing emails and creating sales pages.

A final word on digital products

You now know everything you need to know to start building and selling your own digital products. I have been doing this for over a decade and believe me, there's nothing quite like the feeling of making thousands of sales from a digital item that you can't even hold. Even better, you don't have to deal with customers directly and you can – literally – make money while you sleep. One of my first jobs every morning – as a UK resident – has been to check the US income that I made overnight.

I can't recommend this strategy highly enough. However, you choose to approach it – and that choice is entirely yours – the digital products business will give you a personal, financial and geographical freedom that nothing else can deliver. Since my kids were young, I've been telling them to forget conventional employment and to build themselves a digital business. There's no boss, no corporate nonsense, no pointless office presenteeism, just focused activity making high-value products which create a consistent, ongoing income.

However, you choose to pursue this business I wish you every success with it; the moment you see that first sale coming in, you'll be hooked for life.

ABOUT THE AUTHOR

Hi, I'm Paul Teague and I'm a non-fiction, thriller and science fiction writer from the UK.

I write non-fiction as P. Teague, thrillers as Paul J. Teague and science fiction as Paul Teague.

I'm a former broadcaster and journalist with the BBC, but I have also worked as a primary school teacher, a disc jockey, a shopkeeper, a waiter and a sales rep.

Let's get connected!
https://paulteague.co.uk

Printed in Great Britain
by Amazon